The Matter of Capital

The Matter of Capital

Poetry and Crisis in the American Century

Christopher Nealon

Harvard University Press
Cambridge, Massachusetts
London, England
2011

Printed in the United States of America

Library of Congress Cataloging-in-Publication Data

Nealon, Christopher S. (Christopher Shaun), 1967–
The matter of capital : poetry and crisis in the American century /
Christopher Nealon.
p. cm.
Includes bibliographical references and index.
ISBN 978-0-674-05872-9 (alk. paper)
1. American poetry—20th century—History and criticism.
2. Capitalism and literature. 3. American poetry—21st century—
History and criticism. I. Title.
PS323.5.N43 2011
811'.54093553—dc22 2010029578

Contents

The Matter of Capital

Introduction

The Matter of Capital, or Catastrophe and Textuality

This book argues that the workings of capitalism are a central subject matter of twentieth-century American poetry in English. More specifically, I argue that, across the century, and across aesthetic orientations, a wide variety of poets respond to the social changes wrought by capitalism by making recourse to different ideas of poetry as textual and rhetorical "matter"—a source of varying subject matter, of topics, even of arguments. I mean my title, then, to be a lightly punning analogy to "The Matter of Britain," or "The Matter of France"—the many-authored bodies of writing about King Arthur and Charlemagne, respectively, that name a protagonist larger and more encompassing than any single writer's corpus.[1]

I also mean the analogy in my title to lure us away from an absolute distinction between "form" and "content," because "matter" in the Arthurian and Carolingian cases contains the sense, not only of subject matter, but of subject matter given different forms, and expressed as different kinds of content—abridged, expanded, translated, revised. So "matter," in what follows, will mean for me less a metaphysically substantial "content" lodged in the abstraction of "form" than a question returned to through different topoi, in different forms, and different genres. These imply different senses of what texts are, and who poets are, when brought into the orbit of capital.

My sense of "matter" as topical and as reworkable also points to an important feature of the poetry I'll be considering here, which is how textual—rather than, say, lyrical—its imagination of itself tends to be. Indeed, the strongest commonality among the poets I focus on is a link they all explore between poetry as a textual art and the resources of that textuality for preserving poetry in the face of disaster—hence this chapter's subtitle, "Catastrophe and Textuality." For reasons I will discuss below, it has been difficult for critics to probe the historical imagination that gets attached to the idea of textuality in poetry in English because of the overlap of two critical traditions—a New Critical tradition in which modern poetry has been understood generically, as always gesturing back to an originally oral "lyric" in one sense or another, and a poststructuralist tradition in which the idea of textuality takes on such powerful philosophical overtones that its mundane history is eclipsed.

There is another reason it has been difficult to recognize the textual imaginary of modern poetry in English, which is that the canonical story of the emergence of textual culture in the West, Walter Ong's *Orality and Literacy,* is told as a story of "the technologization of the word." Ong's technical history, with its yearning for a return to the orality of dialectical pedagogy, not only obscures the ongoing coexistence of orality and literacy in textual culture, but also flattens out the differences among the grammatical arts, which encode different understandings of the social functions of texts and of literacy. Recent scholarship in medieval studies, however, has provided a more multifaceted picture of the shifts in the meanings of grammar and rhetoric as they became more enmeshed in textual cultures (Irvine, *The Making of Textual Culture*).

This scholarship also makes clear the enduring link between textual culture and civilizational crisis—not only via the traditional story, by which monastic textual labor preserves the heritage of "western civilization" between the fall of Rome and the rise of Europe, but also by way of the history of the literary arts as mediating agents in the transfer of political power from Greece to Rome and, later, from Rome to the modern European centers of power. As Rita Copeland has shown, these transfers of power demanded tremendous expenditures of skill on textual commentary and translation—between Greek and Latin, and later between Latin and the emergent vernaculars. In each case, concerns about creating literate classes, and developing a literary tradition for an emergent language, made the writing of poetry—which is to say, the copying down of poetry, paraphrasing it, translating it, imitating it—crucial to the advance of the civilizational projects of emergent powers (Copeland, *Rhetoric, Hermeneutics, and Translation*).

So literary "matter" in the sense of the poetic record of heroic deeds has a cousin sense of "matter" as the material practices of making texts. Indeed, Eugene Vance has argued that in the chivalric romances of Chrétien de Troyes we can see a historical movement "from topic to tale"—an incorporation of the projects of the older grammatical arts into an emergent sense of how to depict heroic action *(From Topic to Tale).* My use of the phrase "the matter of capital" depends on such scholarship, along with the work of Ernst Robert Curtius, for help in developing my sense of what "the matter of capital" might mean in twentieth-century American poetry: topics, topoi, and techniques that produce a *textual imaginary* for that poetry, which it uses to stage confrontations between poetry and capital.[2]

As I say, however, the critical models available in the American academy after World War II have made it difficult to discern the existence of this textual imaginary, or even the persistence of capitalism as subject matter for American poetry—notwithstanding the career-long effort of a scholar like Cary Nelson to broaden the canons of American poetry to include poems written from in and around the American labor movement.[3] Before giving you a preliminary sense of the breadth of poetry we might include in the matter of capital, then, I'd like to offer a brief account of why it's been so hard to name.

Virginia Jackson has argued that the professionalization of literary criticism from the time of the New Critics has produced a tendency to read all poems as lyrics, where "lyric" means a record of the voice or the mind speaking to itself, as in T. S. Eliot's conception of the mode *(Dickinson's Misery).* This seems true of New Criticism. But I am also interested in a related phenomenon, which is how, beginning in the 1970s, the language of philosophy stepped in to fill the gap left by New Critical insistence on the aesthetic autonomy of the poem. In the context of the long dominance of New Critical models that insisted that poems needed no external frame by which to be read, the increasingly philosophical approach to the study of poetry in the 1970s and 1980s served as a welcome countermove, an insistence that there was something public, and something intellectual, about poetry, that it was not just grist for the mill of undergraduate composition classes and introductory surveys, and that it could not, and should not, be kept sequestered from the larger questions it raised.

Those questions, however, were themselves complexly determined by the political situation of the era, which was never quite investigated by the new philosophical criticism. This is plainly evident in the strongest criticism from the period, which by my lights was written by Marjorie Perloff and Charles Altieri. Both Perloff and Altieri were at the forefront of the expansion of the poetic canon to include more experimental writing in the 1980s, and both helped turn American poetry criticism away from a reduction of the poetic to the lyrical. Both, too, were indispensable in providing intellectual frameworks by which the "mainstream" of American poetry could articulate what was becoming an emphatic shift to the aesthetic left.

But even this strong work tended merely to name, then draw back from, the conditions that arguably made it urgent to restore to the study of poetry a sense of high intellectual stakes. By those "conditions," I mean both the crises and the triumphs of global capitalism from about 1973 on. These crises have been felt in the trials of poor, working-class, and middle-class people: the end of the post–World War II boom, the return of the business cycle, and the increasingly hysterical speculative bubbles of the 1980s, the 1990s, and the first decade of the twenty-first century, each in its way designed to find outlets for wealth unmoored from the "real" economy. The triumphs have largely been those of the capitalist classes: the defeats of the labor movement in the United States from the Reagan era onward, and the successful capitalization of everyday life, the famous "dematerialization" of labor, or "flexible accumulation" that has meant, not so much the liberation of working people from the demands of wage labor, but the colonization of extramechanical skills by the demands of the market.

These developments are keenly felt in the poetry of the period, as I hope to show; but they are felt and dismissed, or felt and shunted to the side, in the criticism, with the intellectual cost that critics have had nothing other than a cursory account of the history of the twentieth century. Take the case of Perloff, whose work has been indispensable for reframing our sense of the norm by which we recognize "poetry." Perloff argued throughout the 1980s and 1990s that the dominance of the Romantic lyric as a reference point in poetic criticism made much of the most interesting poetic work of the century illegible. She made it possible to see that collage forms—the mixture of verse and prose, or of visual and textual elements, or even the play of chance operations—all were part of a legitimate poetic tradition, one where ideas took precedence over "imagination." She is emphatic that this is a poetry specific to the era: "In the poetry of the late twentieth century, the cry of the heart, as Yeats called it, is increasingly subjected to the play of the mind" (*The Dance of the Intellect,* 197). But she has no account of the history of the century such that it should have produced an idea-driven poetry. Everywhere there are hints of what that history might be; at one point in her pathbreaking 1981 book *The Poetics of Indeterminacy,* she cites the critic James McFarlane's account of modernism as a tension between Symbolist "superintegration" of language, and a breakdown of coherence best rendered by Yeats's "things fall apart"—but what mysterious force might have brought this volatile combination of integration and disintegration into being in the twentieth century is not answered. Elsewhere, pressed by the specifics of a 1979 John Ashbery poem, "Litany," which reflects on the aimless frenzies of an "increasingly mobile populace," Perloff writes, "In this sense, Ashbery's 'hymn to possibility' is indeed a litany for the computer age. If it renounces the phrasal repetition indigenous to the form [of the traditional litany], it is because things no longer happen in precisely the same way twice" (287).

But when did they? These remarks amount to little more than a suggestion that ours has been an especially Heraclitean age. At the end of *The Poetics of Indeterminacy,* Perloff suggests that it's not just the age, but something about America, that generates collaged, indeterminate, nonlyric forms:

> When, in other words, the poetry of indeterminacy, of anti-symbolism, has reached its outer limit, it comes back once more to such basic "literary" elements as the hypnotic sound pattern, the chant, the narrative account, the conceptual scheme. In the poetry of the future, we are likely to find more emphasis on these elements. The so-called "belatedness" of our poetry—belated with respect to the Romantic tradition only—may turn out to be its very virtue. "America," said John Cage, "has an intellectual climate suitable for radical experimentation. We are, as Gertrude Stein said, the oldest country of the twentieth century. And I like to add: in our air way of knowing nowness." (339)

So the sheer present-tense nature of America, its determining position in history, seems to be exemplary of some unnamed process that is both radically disintegrative—it pushes indeterminacy to its "outer limit"—and reintegrative, or possibly "superintegrative," returning again and again to plunder raw materials. What might this mysterious process, so closely identified with America, actually be? The old exceptionalist argument—that we have no medieval past, we are the oldest young country—serves as an explanation that isn't one.

By the early 1990s, the high poetic profile of the Language school had created an even more pressing need for accounts of its historical emergence. But even a wonderful book like Joseph M. Conte's 1991 *Unending Design* fell back on quasi-mythic accounts of language and the material world to account for the rise of Language poetics. Conte's book is immensely clarifying for its account of the importance of open-ended, serial forms to the poetry of the late twentieth century, and he hints at an analogous relationship between this open-endedness and the work of mass production, as when he offers the example of the automobile as an instance of seriality (22, 41). He even notes that Robert Duncan, in a late essay that critiques New Critical models of reading poetry, puts his critique in anticapitalist terms, comparing New Criticism's sense of form to the commodity form. After coming extremely close to the possibility that there is a relationship between capitalism and the emergence of serial forms as a poetic dominant in late-century American poetry, though, Conte retreats to a physical formulation, suggesting that perhaps Language poetry's turn to seriality simply reflects "the many ways beyond the logical and the sequential in which things come together" (280). Elsewhere, Conte offers an alternative rendition, in which

> the traditional lyric speaker who is firmly established and thought to preside over the business of the poems is evicted by a variety of recycled rhetoric, multiple voices to which no priority has been assigned. Without the endorsement of a dominant persona, the language of the poem can be said to speak for itself. (44)

But what does "language," left to speak "for itself," actually say? Might the word "evicted" in this passage carry a trace of the material history by which what scholars think of as modernism became what, less and less often these days, they call "postmodern"? And why is "language itself" speaking now, as opposed to some other time, when it didn't? Questions like these have been begged in American poetry criticism for more than thirty years.

Among the influential poetry scholars in this period, Charles Altieri comes closest to acknowledging the circumstances by which critics became mute in the face of historical crisis, though he does so, not in discussing critics, but in discussing poetry. In this passage from his powerful 1984 book, *Self and Sensibility in Contemporary American Poetry*, Altieri reflects on the revolutionary sixties from the vantage point of the Reagan era. In that decade, he writes,

> poets felt that intense poetic experience might serve as witness and proof of the power of mind to recover numinous values trampled underfoot by the assumptions of liberal industrial society. Now that the desire to transform society, or even to transform long-standing aspects of American personality, has come to seem to many at best escapist and at worst another of the illusions Americans create to avoid the contradictions in their lives, poets have sought quieter, more distinctly personal and relativistic ways of adjusting to what seem inescapable conditions . . .
>
> Ours is an age that must come to terms with failed expectations and, worse, the guilt of recognizing why we held such ambitious dreams. (36–37)

This passage is exemplary of the refusal to think about the role of capital in political and literary history, for two reasons. One is that, in trying to dismiss left-wing political aspirations as psychological flaws, and approvingly citing a turn to "quieter, more distinctly personal and relativistic ways of adjusting to what seem inescapable conditions," Altieri ends up creating the contradiction he thinks this inward turn avoids—a contradiction between the quietude of the inward personal life, rendered as a retreat, and the force required to keep the world away from it. This contradiction has a psychic expression as well, which is the "guilt" that Altieri, with heartbreaking candor, says attaches to having dreamed of a better world. That guilt, like the wall around a gated community, blocks further political thinking by punishing the political thinker for having dared to imagine or to work for revolutionary change.

In mentioning this guilt, Altieri touches on a powerful structure of feeling in American political life, one that has always posed problems for the left, which congeals in the idea that it is a betrayal to think against the system—a betrayal against one's friends, one's community, one's art. Distantly behind this idea lies the real material threat against workers who choose to strike—the possibility that striking would threaten their family's security, or bring down violence on them. Transposed into an academic setting, the idea seems to be that, in developing a critical analysis of capitalism, the critic forsakes daily life, the small beauties; he becomes arrogant, unable to see what's right in front of his nose; or she becomes preachy, solipsistic, hypnotized by abstractions. If one is a critic of poetry, the too-critical critic loses the ability to perform subtle close readings.

And what if one is a poet? This book is not about the resistance to the idea of writing about capitalism. But a glance at some contemporary poetry that takes up that resistance can serve as a handy measure of why, for so long, it has been difficult to name exactly the extent to which many poets *have* written about it. Here is a 2005 poem by the poet Katy Lederer, who gained extrapoetic notice during the financial crisis of 2008–2009 as the "Hedge Fund Poet," because she worked at D.E. Shaw, a private equity firm in New York:

A NIETZSCHEAN REVIVAL
I thought I was almost lost.
Or overwrought.
Or rotten.
As I stroked with quivering fingers this harp,
the tongue-perturbed minions running amok,
their scaffolded ears waiting isolately for the word that would deign to leave heaven.
In the morning, when I manufacture lyrics on these listless keys,
when the money and its happy apparatus do call and lure, do call and lure.
These poets speak of capital as if they have some faint idea.
Capital: a sexy word they read in Marx their freshman year.
I ask you: what do these poets know of capital?
Across its strings, their fingers play a Nietzschean revival.
I envy them their will to power.

(42)

Capitalism, in this poem, is work for experts; poets, whether or not they or their families have lost their mortgages, or their retirement, cannot "know of" it, because they don't work at investment banks. And for a poet to write about capitalism is hubris, or worse, a "will to power" that drowns out the vulnerable harpist, the real poet—notice that her poems are "lyric" poems—who also, by chance, happens to work right at the heart of things, where capital actually resides. All the ugliness is on the side of the critical poets; the movements of money are just a "happy apparatus." The poem could not be more efficient in performing the punishing, all-too-familiar reversal by which critics of capital, not its agents, are imagined as the bringers of violence into the world.

Much subtler is this recent poem by Jennifer Moxley, who more than any poet of her generation has blended a critical position on capitalism with a distaste for taking critical positions (I cite the first and final stanzas):

OUR DEFIANT MOTIVES
And what if we succeed? Then what. What if we,
who are fond of thinking that our lives have been
hindered vigorously by scheming statesmen
and entrepreneurs—scummy down to the one—
find ourselves out on a stretch of open sea
with none but a smooth trajectory
that looks to be of our own making?
. . .
Are we ashamed of our own well-being?
Does it admit of a terrible pact somewhere in our past?
Let's not turn to face the wake, in which some may be
drowning. Rather, let's redraw its rippling "V" to suit
our need to feel that we are the ones who really suffered.
We suffered the most. More than anyone else, for we
understood their suffering, didn't we, and we
were the ones who took it upon ourselves to make it new.

(*Clampdown*, 50–51)

As the poem moves from satirical self-chiding to a deeper self-damning, there emerges an analysis of the flaws of leftist critique in which poets are mocked for accusing "structures" or influential classes of injustice, without their realizing that they do so at the expense of those who "really suffered," whose experience becomes mere material for the modernist transmutations ("make it new") of suffering into negative art. The lancing double meaning of that "make it new"—as in, make suffering into modernism, but also, make others suffer afresh—expresses succinctly enough Moxley's reluctance to participate in what she clearly sees as a ritualized, empty leftism—or, worse, a preening, damaging leftism. Once again, critique is seen as guilty, as an injuring act, one that hurts others more vulnerable than the critic.

In psychological terms, it is hard to imagine a more durable twentieth-century victory for the right than the persistence of this structure of feeling, which dates at least to the 1930s, and the international left's horrified disavowal of Stalinism. This argumentativeness mutates in the Cold War, when anti-Communist liberal intellectuals, not least major figures like

Albert Camus and Hannah Arendt, successfully equate communism with fascism via the portmanteau concept of totalitarianism. They also pave the way for the poststructuralist critique of "totalizing" thought that became so popular in the U.S. academy in the 1980s and 1990s, as though it were the critic who tried to name the totalizing work of capital, rather than capital, who was failing to do justice to particulars, or to aesthetic experience.[4]

For a poet like Moxley, the response to the suffering born of the scheming of "statesmen" and "entrepreneurs" is to look away, and to damn herself and her compatriots for doing so. As we will see, this dynamic of "looking away" from suffering and cursing oneself for doing it will have a crucial role to play in the poetry of John Ashbery, the subject of my second chapter. Ashbery, like Moxley, is keenly aware of what it is, precisely, he's looking away *from*—in his case, something like the consolidation of capitalist spectacle in 1970s New York. But poetry criticism—not only of Ashbery, but of the poetry of the last third of the century—seems not to notice the agony in the turning away, or not to notice it at all, or silently to assent to it. So Perloff, in her 1996 *Wittgenstein's Ladder*, champions the philosophy of Wittgenstein as an analogy to the writing of the Language poets, because Wittgenstein's sense of language as a closed game allows for the possibility of making the everyday and the ordinary become strange. But she ignores the Language poets' own account of why the "ordinary" and the "everyday" were so important to them in the 1980s—not just because it was a countermove to the use of high-literary language, but also because they saw the language of making the ordinary into the strange as a counterlanguage to the amplified messages of the state and the mass media.

Altieri, meanwhile, in his *Painterly Abstraction in Modernist American Poetry* of 1995, adopts a defeated, Boethian attitude toward the relationship between poetry and mass spectacle, sympathetically viewing "postmodern" poetry as consigned to the consolations of a Kantian philosophy in which one tests one's capacities to judge within the carefully delimited, ever-narrowing space of what "politics" has not yet tainted. As he puts it:

> In my view, these Postmodernist experiments introduce a substantially new spiritual dispensation, finally making it possible to imagine an art that does not set itself against apparently irresistible forces of social and historical change . . .

> The more we see what the task of accommodation involves, the more we shall need to challenge the contemporary imagination, by reminding it of those moments when the mind sees itself as capable of living in, and for, communities not bound to that history and the compromises it entails. We must continue to seek ideals of identity that insist on making their own forms for the noise threatening to subsume all of our fictions into the world that is all too much with us. (379)

Reading Altieri's melancholic tribute to restricted action, and Perloff's amiable celebration of the bounded linguistic space of the everyday, it is easy to see why Adorno, in his lectures on Kant's *Critique of Pure Reason,* remarked about Kantian critique that "what has been codified in *The Critique of Pure Reason* is a theodicy of bourgeois life which is conscious of its own practical activity while despairing of the fulfillment of its own utopia" (6). In Altieri's case in particular, this theodicy operates as a transposition by which political defeats for the left (the defeat of "the desire to transform society") mutate into a defeat *by politics,* by the encroachment of "the political" per se into the domain of the aesthetic.

Work like Altieri's and Perloff's thus gave us a powerfully depoliticizing language for poetry in the 1980s and 1990s. Ironically, the critical language of that period that most often kept some version of politics in view for American readers of poetry—that is, the language of French poststructuralism—comes around to making its own versions of these depoliticizing moves. This work has been more commanding in comparative literature departments than in English departments, partly because it is built around a European canon of poetry. But it has had wide influence on American work, both for the way its structuralist heritage makes it possible to think of poetry in terms of a seemingly cross-disciplinary notion of textuality, as opposed to a merely literary vocabulary of genre or mode, and for how it invites critics to imagine the relationship between poetry and politics.

This invitation involves, on the French side, subtle analogies between philosophical arguments and political history; and, on the American side, a transposition of those analogies into a different academic and political scene. So it is hard to describe their influence without pausing for a bit over the details of how such theoretical arguments actually tended to look on the ground. One might take any of a variety of examples, but I think the work of Jacques Derrida is especially important here. Over the course of his long career, Derrida revised his thinking about literature, philosophy, and politics countless times, but his early work is very clear in establishing a set of founding relays among those domains. So I'd like to slow down for a moment and take a look at his influential 1966 essay "From Restricted to General Economy: A Hegelianism without Reserve." The essay leans on Alexandre Kojève's Marxian interpretation of Hegel in order to produce an allegory of Hegelian negativity as labor, then, enabled by this analogy or allegory, turns to Bataille and a Kierkegaardian absurdism to argue that the negative must be understood in terms other than those to which philosophy submits it; the negative, for Derrida, is constantly being brought into philosophical service—exploited, he suggests—as the other of meaning, providing the prompt to philosophical concept honing. But it cannot be assimilated to such uses.

Derrida's essay makes two key moves that, taken together, proved extremely persuasive on American shores. One is to transpose the question of the exploitation of labor into a philosophical register, by reading it as the capture and exploitation of negativity by philosophy, where it is forced into the work of systematic thinking. The other is to suggest that the true character of the negative is expressed in chance, and in play, and that this true character of the negative is best understood in literary terms—or, more specifically, modernist poetic terms, best exemplified by Mallarmé's *Un coup de dés jamais n'abolira le hasard.* Derrida gestures at Mallarmé's poem this way:

> The poetic or ecstatic is that *in every discourse* which can open itself up to the absolute loss of its sense, to the (non-)base of the sacred, of nonmeaning, of un-knowledge or play, to the swoon from which it is reawakened by a throw of the dice. (261)

This move is significant because, having established the question of labor as a philosophical question of negativity, and having posited the modernist poetics of Mallarmé as a privileged site for the expression of the negativity that philosophy seeks to capture, Derrida aligns the poetic specificity of the modernist lyric with the uncapturable life force of the rebellious worker. He contrasts the "master" of Hegel's master-slave dialectic with a Bataillean "sovereign" who laughs at philosophy's mere "amortization" of the negative, who laughs at death: "laughter alone exceeds dialectics and the dialectician" (256). Noting that "philosophy is work *itself* for Bataille," he adds that Hegelian *Aufhebung* is "laughable" because it is merely a "*busying* of discourse" that starts panting as it "reappropriates all negativity for itself" (252, 257). Philosophy, as the essay unfolds, is "work itself" in the sense that it is a set of operations that *compel* work, that force the negative to produce meaning and knowledge, and that bustles about breathlessly as it mistakenly thinks it is achieving "knowledge" in the process. "Philosophy"—that is, Hegelian philosophy, *Aufhebung*, the dialectic—"philosophy," in this allegory, is a bourgeois.

Now the bourgeoisie, as a mercantile or a professional class, are not entirely, or not necessarily, the same as the industrial capitalist class that actually *would* compel labor; so we should note a slight shift or transposition in the Marxian critique here. Similarly, note that it is not capital, but the dialectic, that is the enemy—so that the militant worker, when the moment of rebellion finally becomes possible, rebels not against capital but against philosophy. Indeed, at the moment when Derrida's allegory depicts rebellion, "the negative"—figured, Derrida says, in the Hegelian slave, who Derrida says Kojève suggests is the worker (276)—at the moment of rebellion, the worker looks more existential than militant. Indeed, he looks more like a Resistance fighter in World War II than a proletarian. Here Derrida has been discussing the merely philosophical revolutions of Kant and Hegel, who can be credited with discovering the philosophical import of the negative, but who made the mistake of "[taking it] seriously." By contrast, he suggests, for Bataille, the negative (here, again, personified) is more truly radical, to the point of its utter transformation:

> [It] can no longer be called negative precisely because it has no reserved underside, because it can no longer permit itself to be converted into positivity, it can no longer *collaborate* with the continuous linking-up of meaning, concept, time, and truth in discourse; because it literally can no longer *labor* and let itself be interrogated as "the work of the negative." (259–260)

Note the italicized word "collaborate" in this passage, which to my ear is a giveaway signal that the allegory of the negative-as-worker has now received an overlay of wartime militancy. The italicization of the word "labor" signals the blending of the two background personifications, wound even tighter together by the word "interrogated," which links the refusal of the worker and the developing militance of the resistance fighter in a pun on the interrogative.

What all these deft allegorical, anthropomorphic, and transposing gestures accomplish, for Derrida, is the insight that German dialectical philosophy is no match for French literary modernism:

> In interpreting negativity as labor, in betting for discourse, meaning, history, etc., Hegel has bet against play, against chance. He has blinded himself . . . to the fact that play *includes* the work of meaning or the meaning of work. (260)

In 1966 this overlay of the figure of the militant Resistance fighter on top of the figure of the worker, who is cannier than the philosopher-bourgeois about the work-canceling play that modern poetry highlights, is a kind of backward glance. But it is also an echo of a contemporary development in French politics. Here is a key passage from the 1966 Situationist pamphlet *On the Poverty of Student Life*:

> For the proletariat revolt is a festival or it is nothing: in revolution the road of excess leads to the palace of wisdom. A palace which knows only one rationality: the game. The rules are simple: to live instead of devising a lingering death, and to indulge untrammeled desire. (S. Ford 116)

The distribution of this pamphlet by the students of the University of Strasbourg helped trigger, two years later, the student alliance with workers in the uprisings of May 1968; and it remains an exemplary text for non-Communist Party, Marxist anticapitalism in France. I cannot trace the lines of commonality or influence between Derrida and the Situationists with much precision here; it is hard to say whether Derrida is leaning on rebellious student energies, or the students are picking up on something that Derrida is also aware of, a critique of Communist Party politics that is registered as a romantic (here, Blakean) critique of Hegel (the "lingering death" of the dialectic as work, as opposed to "untrammeled desire," which Derrida renders, in the title of his essay, as "Hegelianism without reserve").

Is Derrida, in 1966, politicizing philosophy or academicizing Situationist politics? Impossible to say; more easy to recognize is that the leveraging of modernist poetry into an antidialectical argument with Hegel (and implicitly, doctrinaire, party-line Marxism) becomes *the* gesture into which the idea of "poetry" is incorporated in the French theory that traveled to American shores in the 1970s and 1980s. This antidialecticism is emphatically present in Julia Kristeva's 1974 *Revolution in Poetic Language,* which pits the disruptive literary practice of Mallarmé and Lautréamont against a psychoanalytic subject falsely unified by the state and society. And it organizes Jean-Luc Nancy's 1982 *The Inoperative Community*, which cites Bataille's remark from *Literature and Evil* that "literature cannot assume the task of directing collective necessity," in order to position a Levinasian-Heideggerian understanding of poetry as an "interruption" against both those literary texts that seek after mere produced beauty and that Marxism that imagines "productivity" as the only engine of history.[5] This is not to mention the work of Gilles Deleuze and Félix Guattari, or, more recently, Alain Badiou, who have all kept alive, from very different philosophical positions, the practice of pitting one literary modernism or another against a cartoon of Hegel made to stand in for something like either the rigidness or the insufficient militancy of the French Communist Party.

In 1986 it was already possible for a canny observer like Andreas Huyssen to observe of the "postmodern" theory being consumed in the United States that "rather than offering a *theory of postmodernity* and developing an analysis of contemporary culture, French theory provides us primarily with an *archeology of modernity*, a theory of modernism at the stage of its exhaustion" (*After the Great Divide*, 209). To this it seems useful to add that, along with an "archeology of modernity," French theory offered American literary critics a philosophical allegory of postwar French politics, centered by and large on a tiny canon of writers—Mallarmé, Baudelaire, Rimbaud, Hölderlin and Celan—whose modernist extremity (or, in the case of Hölderlin, his modernism *avant la lettre*) converts that political allegory into an allegory of the war between literature and philosophy.[6] I would suggest that in the absence of a powerful American Communist Party, or an American Situationism, or a sustained American argument with Hegel, this allegorical war of the disciplines (poetry versus philosophy) comes to explain the meaning or significance of "poetry" in those flanks of the American literary academy that tilt in a continental direction. Though it has a very different provenance than the American criticism that sequesters poetry against the noise of the spectacle, then, American consumption of the political allegories of French theory amounts to a similar sequestration, where "literature" and "poetry" signify a realm of existentialist, or absurdist, or monist freedom that the dialectic cannot capture.

Something different, but related, happens in the postwar history of German-language stylistic analysis of poetry, which, primarily through the work of Theodor Adorno, has had broad influence on American thinking about the relationship of poetry to capitalism. The German tradition of poetry criticism, devolving from the work of Curtius, is more philological than philosophical, and less interested in foregrounding the canon of literary modernism than in establishing stylistic analyses that extend to premodern periods. But it is strongly interested in the question of the individual's relation to the masses, as when Erich Auerbach highlights the emergence of the Christian sermon in late antiquity as a kind of "mass movement" that does not erase but prizes each individual, or when Adorno frames the modernity of the lyric under capitalism as the struggle of the isolated poet, by withdrawing himself from society, to preserve something socially free that exists only in potential.[7] I would like to take a moment to highlight some of the things American critics have learned from this tradition, but also to show how it comes around, in Adorno, to a stance that is closer to the stance of French poststructuralism than at first appears.

One of the major achievements of the German tradition of poetry criticism is to demonstrate that the postclassical history of literary writing, even when we factor in wide variability around what "the literary" had meant since the classical era, is bound up with the imagination of historical change and civilizational crisis. Hans-Robert Jauss has written comprehensively on how the idea of "the modern," for instance, links historical writing, humanist scholarship, poetry, and aesthetics in a conversation about the meanings of the present in relation to different understandings of history; reading his work, it becomes possible to see the method by which Ezra Pound, T. S. Eliot, and Charles Olson draw parallels and contrasts between ancient and modern figures as a reworking and continuation of an older historiographical and literary-critical genre, the "parallel," which itself has ancient origins, and becomes a central genre for debates about modernity in the late seventeenth-century French *Querelle des anciens et des modernes* ("Modernity and Literary Tradition," 347). One of the fascinating things about Jauss's survey of the literary idea of "the modern" is that, in the history he traces for the term, it mutates from a static term of opposition to ancientness (as in the *Querelle*) to what, by the middle of the nineteenth century, he sees as a term that perpetually "repels itself" in what is experienced by Stendhal and then Baudelaire as the onward rush of historical events. This latter experience, of course, is one way to describe the experience of time in commodity capitalism, as a perpetual rush to the new; what Jauss's survey illuminates is the way in which the aesthetics of modernity we have come to associate with Baudelaire (and, since Baudelaire, Walter Benjamin) have a long genealogy that extends at least as far back as early Christian distinctions around the "modernity" of the Christian era.

The enduring persistence of problems of historical consciousness for literature is not only a question of how literary writing has developed understandings of periods and of the meanings of periodization; it has also attached itself to questions of literary style. The best-known example of this historiographical-stylistic link is Auerbach's argument that, after Augustine, the ancient correlation of kinds of subject matter with degrees of stylistic elevation was disrupted both by the need to preach of high matters to masses of less-educated people, and by a doctrinal sense that Christ's resurrection brought the high low and made the low high. For Auerbach, a Ciceronian low style, or *sermo humilis,* is reworked by Augustine and others into a something like a "humble style" where high and low stylistic registers can mix because the theme of humility is, in Christian preaching and apologetics, also always the theme of sublimity *(Literary Language).* Helplessly, though, this style mixing also obtains a historical-thematic element as well—*sermo humilis* in the Christian tradition also comes to signify being post-Roman, an after-the-fall humility that is historical as well as theological. Down to the twentieth century, then, one of the available functions of style mixing is to index catastrophic historical change on the model of the fall of Rome: Adorno's bravura mixture of essayistic and philosophical writing in the post-Holocaust volume *Minima Moralia* is a good example, because its title not only inverts the praise orientation of Plutarch's *Moralia,* but also points to Gregory the Great's *Moralia in Job,* a signal instance for Auerbach of *sermo humilis.*

Indeed, Adorno's writing on poetry foregrounds its relation to historical catastrophe at every turn, though his American readers have often taken his writing to demonstrate generic truths about lyric intensity or compression as defining specificities of poetry. Unfortunately, Adorno himself facilitates this drift in the direction of generic reading, both when he remarks in *Negative Dialectics* that he may have been wrong to say that it is barbaric to write poetry after Auschwitz, given that "perennial suffering has just as much right to find expression as a victim of torture has to scream" (355), and when, in "Lyric Poetry and Society," he refers to the lyric poem as a "philosophical sundial of history" (221). These remarks have often been taken to mean that there is something generically special about the lyric's intensity or its linguistic compression, but in formulating them—especially the second remark—Adorno leans on and reworks the tradition of stylistics in which literature is understood as gradually developing an idiomatic historiographical function, not only an ahistorical "intensity." In "Lyric Poetry and Society," for instance, Adorno turns to the poetry of Stefan George, whose compressed style he reads as an allegory of the generation of an older class imaginary out of the emergence of a new one:

> While George's poetry—that of the splendidly individual—presupposes as a condition of its very possibility an individualistic, bourgeois society, and the individual who exists for himself alone, it nevertheless bans the commonly accepted forms, no less than the themes, of bourgeois poetry. Because this poetry, however, can speak from no other standpoint or configuration than precisely those bourgeois frames of mind which it rejects . . . because of this it is blocked, dammed at the source: and so it feigns a feudal condition. (224–225)

George's success, like the success Auerbach imagines for Christian *sermo humilis,* emerges from rejecting a high rhetoric:

> Elevated style is attained not by pretending to rhetorical figures and rhythms, but by ascetically omitting whatever would lessen the distance from the tainted language of commerce. In order that the subject may truly resist the lonely process of reification he may not even attempt anymore to retreat into himself—to his private property. He is frightened by the traces of an individualism which has meanwhile sold itself to the literary supplements of the marketplace. The poet must, rather, by denying himself, step out of himself. (226)

This dazzling passage, which has been so influential in developing an understanding of the political value of the lyric poem, nonetheless limits our understanding of the relationship between poetry and capitalism to the negative: the lyric's compression and intensity are a sacrificial austerity, or a scream, and the rejections such stances or cries signify become a definition of the lyric—not least the lyric as "philosophical sundial of history." But the work of Jauss and others suggests that if the poem is a sundial of history, this is because the history of the literary is in part the history of the generation of historiographical metaphors (standing on the shoulders of giants; postcatastrophic lowness) like the metaphor of the sundial in the first place. And when Adorno situates a poet like George in the heritage of *poésie pure*—"this follower of Mallarmé," Adorno calls him—his work ends up reinforcing the figures of renunciation and sequestration that postwar French and American thinking about poetry have also privileged as the way to think about poetry and capitalism.

So where the key critics of American poetry of the last twenty years have chosen not to write about the relation of that poetry to capitalism, the French and German critical traditions most widely referred to in the United States have encouraged ways of thinking about that relation that tend to imply that poetic writing is prima facie political, or that the only significant relation between a poem and capitalism is rigorous eschewal.

But the record of the actual poetry of the twentieth century does not bear out this claim, and I would like to take some time in the next several pages to suggest as much. Even if we narrowed our sense of "the matter of capital" to include poetry primarily from within an academic canon, we could draw examples from every major "school" of American poetry from the early twentieth century onward. Capital-as-subject-matter appears in Whitmanian guise in Carl Sandburg's 1916 *Chicago Poems*, as in "Masses," where Sandberg writes:

> And then one day I got true look at the Poor, millions of the Poor, patient and toiling; more patient than the crags, tides, and stars; innumerable, patient as the darkness of night—and all broken, humble ruins of nations. (*Collected Poems*, 6)

It appears in elegiac form as poets register the transformation of rural and small-town life by new property relations—not only in the poetry of, say, Robert Frost, but even among the personae of Edgar Lee Masters's *Spoon River Anthology*, as in the poem "'Butch' Weldy," whose protagonist suffers an industrial accident and finds his boss is not liable (19–20).

Later, in the atmosphere of solidarity with the working classes that many poets felt in the 1930s, writers like Muriel Rukeyser developed genre-mixing forms of documentary poetics to capture the costs and the violence of industrial capitalism, as in Rukeyser's pivotal 1938 "The Book of the Dead," which tries to establish a political and literary frame for the deaths by acute silicosis of hundreds of West Virginia coal miners. In the poems from that sequence, Rukeyser begins an attempt to foreground both the media of perception that risk glossing over the miners' tragedy, and the generic pressures that urge both reader and writer to take the political situation and rewrite it in generically recognizable terms—not least as "tragic":

And in the beerplace on the other sidewalk
always one's harsh night eyes over the beerglass
follow the waitress and the yellow apron.
. . .
What do you want—a cliff over a city?
A foreland, sloped to sea and overgrown with roses?
These people live here.[8]

(*Selected Poems*, 31)

Other early and midcentury poetries worked out the problem what frame or angle of approach to use in writing about capitalism by developing languages that strove to correlate poetic and social objectivity. In the work of the loosely aligned Objectivists, this could mean an attempt to capture Marxist theory in verse form, as in Louis Zukofsky's *A:*

The measure all use is time congealed labor
In which abstraction things keep no resemblance
To goods created

(106)

The attempt to correlate poetic and social objectivity could also mean making an attempt to reclaim language from perceived distortions caused by capitalist social relations, as in this section of George Oppen's "A Language of New York":

Possible
To use
Words provided one treat them
As enemies.
Not enemies—Ghosts
Which have run mad
In the subways
And of course the institutions
And the banks. If one captures them
One by one proceeding
Carefully they will restore
I hope to meaning
And to sense.

(*New Collected Poems*, 116)

After World War II, the emergence of the United States as a global superpower consolidated New York's claim to be, not only a financial capital, but also the leading edge of modern artistic energies. In poetry like Frank O'Hara's, the new cosmopolitan possibilities created by these changes allow for an unprecedented and exuberant embrace of mass and popular culture in poetry, and a tentative alignment of mass cultural pleasures with the intimacies of coterie social relationships:

> Lana Turner has collapsed!
> I was trotting along and suddenly
> it started raining and snowing
> and you said it was hailing
> but hailing hits you on the head
> hard so it was really snowing and
> raining and I was in such a hurry
> to meet you but the traffic
> was acting exactly like the sky
> and suddenly I see a headline
> LANA TURNER HAS COLLAPSED!
> there is no snow in Hollywood
> there is no rain in California
> I have been to lots of parties
> and acted perfectly disgraceful
> but I never actually collapsed
> oh Lana Turner we love you get up
>
> (*Selected Poems*, 234)

In this giddy moment, cosmopolitan and populist impulses work side by side to produce a poetry that seems to be able to meet capitalism face-to-face, unafraid, even to see it as benign. In a heartbeat O'Hara can

> have a hamburger and a malted and buy
> an ugly NEW WORLD WRITING to see what the poets
> in Ghana are doing these days
>
> (*Selected Poems*, 155)

or proudly note, "I wear workshirts to the opera, / often" (91).

But even O'Hara, who synthesized cosmopolitan and populist impulses more thoroughly than any poet of the century, was uneasy about the divisions of labor enabling those impulses, and that uneasiness registered throughout his career, not only in the famous frenzy of a late poem like "Biotherm," but also in earlier poems like "Interior (with Jane)," which probes the question of those uneasily masked relationships by way of a conceit about the division of labor, not between people, but between people and things:

The eagerness of objects to
be what we are afraid to do
cannot help but move us Is
this willingness to be a motive
in us what we reject? The
really stupid things, I mean
a can of coffee, a 35¢ ear
ring, a handful of hair, what
do these things do to us?

(21)

This ambivalence about the object world created by capitalism is also the subject of Allen Ginsberg's 1955 poem "A Supermarket in California." In that poem Ginsberg struggles, as O'Hara struggled, to maintain a sense of exuberance about the abundant variety of goods he finds in the market, even as he is drawn into melancholy elegy for a "lost America":

What thoughts I have of you tonight, Walt Whitman, for
I walked down the sidestreets under the trees with a headache
self-conscious looking at the full moon.
In my hungry fatigue, and shopping for images, I went
into the neon fruit supermarket, dreaming of your enumerations!
What peaches and what penumbras! Whole families shopping at
night! Aisles full of husbands! Wives in the avocados, babies in the
tomatoes!—and you, Garcia Lorca, what were you doing down by the
watermelons?
I saw you, Walt Whitman, childless, lonely old grubber,
poking among the meats in the refrigerator and eyeing the grocery
boys.
I heard you asking questions of each: Who killed the pork chops?
What price bananas? Are you my Angel?

I wandered in and out of the brilliant stacks of cans following you,
and followed in my imagination by the store detective.
We strode down the open corridors together in our solitary fancy
tasting artichokes, possessing every frozen delicacy, and never
passing the cashier.

(*Selected Poems*, 59)

Ginsberg's self-positioning as lonely, joyous vagrant taps into a hobo imaginary that dates at least back to Whitman's era; and the quietly gay genealogy he constructs by addressing Whitman and including García Lorca in his vision draws on the Popular Front energies of the 1930s, when literary and political genealogy-making became a part of anticapitalist "culture." On the West Coast, those genealogical energies are most fully expressed in the work of Kenneth Rexroth (who admired the youthful Ginsberg in his old age). Here, for instance, are the closing lines of Rexroth's "August 22, 1939"—a date that marks, not the buildup to World War II, as poems like Auden's "September 1, 1939" have taught us to expect, but the anniversary of the execution of the anarchists Nicola Sacco and Bartolomeo Vanzetti:

Dante was homesick, the Chinese made an art of it,
So was Ovid and many others,
Pound and Eliot amongst them,
Kropotkin dying of hunger,
Berkman by his own hand,
Fanny Baron biting her executioners,
Mahkno in the odor of calumny,
Trotsky, too, I suppose, passionately, after his fashion.
Do you remember?
What is it all for, this poetry,
This bundle of accomplishment
Put together with so much pain?
Do you remember the corpse in the basement?
What are we doing at the turn of our years,
Writers and readers of the liberal weeklies?

(*Complete Poems*, 162)

The directness of Rexroth's final turn to his readers is reworked, long after the demise of Popular Front cultural politics, in the writing affiliated with the new social movements of the 1960s, where it serves to mediate difficult questions about the relationship between personal or collective identity, on the one hand, and the workings of capitalism, on the other. The poems of Amiri Baraka are especially noteworthy in this regard; even in early work, Baraka used a strongly personalized mode to express doubts about the cross-class alliances that seemed to hold together the culture of Greenwich Village bohemia, as in this satirical sketch, "A Poem for Speculative Hipsters":

> He had got, finally,
> to the forest
> of motives. There were no
> owls, or hunters. No Connie Chatterleys
> resting beautifully
> on their backs, having casually
> brought socialism
> to England.
>   Only ideas,
> and their opposites.
>   Like,
>   he was *really*
>   nowhere.

(*Transbluesency*, 110)

Later in his career, after he encountered the languages of black self-love and self-hatred developed by the Black Power movement, Baraka returned to the mode of the character sketch, this time to depict black aspirations to success in capitalism as racial betrayal:

> "BLACK BOURGEOISIE"
> has a gold tooth
> sits long hours on a stool
> thinking about money
> . . . .
> has a good word to say
> never says it
> does not hate ofays
> hates instead him-
> self, him black self.

In a poem like "Three Modes of History and Culture," however, Baraka abandons the puncturing satirical sketch as he tries to capture both the systemic and the intangible aspects of the Great Migration of black laborers from the agrarian South to the industrial North. In terms that foreshadow later critical discussions of black culture, not least Houston Baker's idea of a "blues matrix," Baraka co-locates the imperatives of the labor market and the ineffability of song:[9]

> Trains
> leaning north, catching hellfire in windows, passing through
> the first ignoble cities of missouri, to illinois, and the panting Chicago.
> And then all ways, we go where flesh is cheap. Where factories
> sit open, burning the chiefs. Make your way! Up through fog and
>   history
> Make your ways, and swing the general, that it come flash open
> and spill the innards of that sweet thing we heard, and gave theory to.
> (*Transbluesency*, 117)

So Baraka tries to understand capitalism in poetry, not only by way of personalizing strategies, but also in attempts to depict large-scale systemic activity. This movement between the personal and the systemic is mirrored in other social movement poetry of the sixties and seventies, not least in the great outpouring of feminist writing from that period. As with Rexroth and Baraka, Adrienne Rich's feminist work contains a strong drive to recover lost histories, to name the names of ancestors. Unlike those two poets, though, Rich reads the work of historical recovery, which she sees as a necessary part of developing a feminist consciousness, as itself a kind of labor. In poems from the seventies like "Diving into the Wreck" (1973) and "Natural Resources" (1977), Rich creates allegories of historical recovery and becoming conscious that position the feminist subject as deep-sea diver and coal miner—risk takers and danger workers, plunging underground and undersea to discover courage there:

> We are, I am, you are
> by cowardice or courage
> the one who find our way
> back to this scene
> carrying a knife, a camera
> a book of myths

in which
our names do not appear.

(*Diving into the Wreck*, 24)

and:

I have to cast my lot with those
who age after age, perversely,
with no extraordinary power,
reconstitute the world.

(*The Dream of a Common Language*, 67)

After the giddy release of feminist energies in the seventies, Rich's analogy of the feminist subject to risk taker and high-risk laborer gave way to the problem of the vicissitudes of solidarity, of how to "cast [one's] lot" with others. By the 1980s, she was rereading Marx through the lens of the failures of the revolutionary movements of the prior decade, and asking about what prevented "identity politics" from confronting the systemic forces of capital—which, as she puts it in a 2001 essay, "lost no time in rearranging itself around this phenomenon called 'feminism.'" She concludes that "only a politics of the whole society can resist such assimilation" (*Arts of the Possible*, 153).

In the 1990s and the first decade of the twenty-first century, Rich refashioned the sense of heroic smallness that animated her earlier poems into tropes of "conversation," a move that both opened a wider channel between her prose and her poetry and allowed her to maintain a sense that, in an era of right-wing triumphs, intimate relationships and friendships can still nurture revolutionary thinking. The "matter of capital," for Rich, lies in what people say to each other:

In those years, people will say, we lost track
of the meaning of we, of you
we found ourselves
reduced to I
and the whole thing became
silly, ironic, terrible:
we were trying to live a personal life
and, yes, that was the only life
we could bear witness to
But the great dark birds of history screamed and plunged into our
personal weather

They were headed somewhere else
but their beaks and pinions dove
along the shore, through the rages of fog
where we stood, saying I.

(*Dark Fields of the Republic,* 4)

Elsewhere, in a poem sequence called "A Long Conversation" from her 1999 volume *Midnight Salvage,* Rich meditates on the dialogue "between persistence and impatience" in social movements—not least, she seems to suggest, in the queer movement, where "intimate resistance" so often threatens to become merely private rejection (54). Toward the end of the poem, Rich mixes type forms in order to try to capture something like the relationship between "intimate resistance" and blaring spectacle in an era in which solidarity was being beaten back:

the words barely begin
to match the desire
and the mouth crammed with dollars doesn't testify
. . . the eye has become a human eye
when its object has become a human, social object
BRECHT BECOMES GERMAN ICON ANEW
FORGIVEN MARXIST IDEAS

(65)

This trope of a capitalist mismatch between the small and the large, the whispered and the shouted, finds a place in the poetry of the other great social movement of the seventies, the environmental movement. As in feminism, environmentalist activism begins with a capacious intellectual framework that includes forthright critiques of capital, gradually evolves into a more liberal-centrist movement that is institution- rather than grassroots-driven, and then, toward the turn of the millennium, finds elder poet-spokespeople who insist on the return of the question of capitalism to movement discourse.[10] Where latter-day feminism has found a poetic elder stateswoman in Rich, for environmentalists it is figures like Wendell Berry who marshal the resources of poetry as part of insisting on the revival of the critique of capital. Like Rich, who describes politics and poetry as "arts of the possible," Berry insists that the arts, rather than technical knowledge, prepare us to think through the economic and political problems of the day. As he puts it,

> we may have to remove some of the emphasis we have lately placed on science and technology and have a new look at the arts. For an art does not propose to enlarge itself by limitless extension but rather to enrich itself within bounds that are accepted prior to the work. ("Faustian Economics")

This philosophy of economics as an art of limits takes on Horatian and biblical tones in Berry's anticapitalist poetry, as in this poem of the mid-seventies, "Manifesto: The Mad Farmer Liberation Front":

> Love the quick profit, the annual raise,
> vacation with pay. Want more
> of everything ready-made. Be afraid
> to know your neighbors and to die.
> And you will have a window in your head.
> Not even your future will be a mystery
> any more. Your mind will be punched in a card
> and shut away in a little drawer.
> When they want you to buy something
> they will call you. When they want you
> to die for profit they will let you know.
> So, friends, every day do something
> that won't compute. Love the Lord.
> Love the world. Work for nothing.
> Take all that you have and be poor.
> Love someone who does not deserve it.
>
> (*The Mad Farmer Poems*, 12)

Though it tilts left, this poetry is also the product of a southern agrarian populism that was first built around resentment of the industrial North, and it tends to be gender-traditional and nationalist in its advice to readers (the poem also advises, "So long as women do not go cheap / for power, please women more than men," and "Denounce the government and embrace / the flag"). So Berry's "Mad Farmer," doing things that "won't compute," has affinities with the French poststructuralist "schizo" of the same period, but also with the caustic, formal southern gentleman in John Crowe Ransom's 1924 poem "Prometheus in Straits," pretending to be unrefined for the benefit of a northern political and cultural elite whom he deeply resents.[11]

On the West Coast, the poetry of environmentalist activism found its great spokesman in Gary Snyder, who figures the relationship between political power and the land, or money and the land, quite differently than Berry does. Where for the Berry of "Manifesto" the poet's advice is to act so as not to "compute," for Snyder it's money itself that doesn't compute. Berry's economic advice for anticapitalist madmen is framed, as I've said, by the biblical rhetoric of charity ("Take all that you have and be poor" alongside "Love someone who does not deserve it"); Snyder, steeped in the traditions of Zen Buddhism, thinks of money as an enmeshing delusion. In a poem called "Money Goes Upstream" from the 1983 volume *Axe Handles,* Snyder writes:

> There are people who do business within the law.
> And others, who love speed, danger,
> Tricks, who know how to
> Twist arms, get fantastic wealth,
> Hurt with heavy shoulders of power,
> And then drink to it!
>   they don't get caught.
>   they *own* the law.
> Is this reason? Or is it a dream.
> I can smell the grass, feel the stones with bare feet
>   though I sit here shod and clothed
>   with all the people. That's my power.
> And some odd force in this world
> *Not* a power
> That seeks to own the source.
> It dazzles us and it slips us by,
> It swims upstream.
>
> (101–102)

I'd like to close my preliminary survey of the poetic matter of capital with Snyder, because the contrast between his and Berry's sense of what money is raises a question about poetry that I think subtends all the poems I've mentioned so far, and that poses a central problem for the poems I'll be reading most closely in the rest of this book. For both Berry and Snyder, money is the vehicle for the political power of a "they," a class of people who can compel others. For Berry this power derives from a vision of money as substantial, as something that can be divested from as well as invested;

but for Snyder, money's power—not, he says, even properly a "power"—derives from its insubstantiality, its "dazzle" and ungraspability.

Lodged in this problem of what kind of matter money is, is the question of what kind of matter poetry is. This is not to say that Berry and Snyder, or any of the other poets I've surveyed here, take the problem of social relations under capitalism to be entirely reducible to the problem of the character of money. But the question of money's substantiality posed in these poems points directly to the question of what poetry is, or would have to be, in order to be opposed to capital: equally substantial, or equally insubstantial? Fleet and circulatory, like money, or defiantly valueless, money's opposite? Imitative of the movements that produce crisis and rushing headlong into it, or built to survive crisis and live on into a postcapitalist future?

These contradictory paths mark out some of the key poetic attitudes to capital of the last century; often they are found fully opposed in the work of a single poet. This brings me to the poetry I'll be discussing in the following chapters. All of the poets I consider have at the center of their literary projects an attempt to understand the relationship between poetry and capitalism, most often worked out as an attempt to understand the relationship of texts to historical crisis. I look at a variety of writing from across the century—from Pound and Auden, in Chapter 1, to John Ashbery in Chapter 2, Jack Spicer and the Language poets in Chapter 3, and the contemporary writers Claudia Rankine and Kevin Davies in Chapter 4. In each case I try to locate their work in the context of a historical and economic crisis: the economic disasters and the crises of parliamentary democracy that marked the interwar years; the early neoliberal experiments that produced a forced restructuring of New York City's economic and cultural life in the 1970s; the emergence of nuclear threat in the Cold War and its mutation into the crisis of American hegemony in the Vietnam era; and the threats of mass poverty and environmental disaster that mark the speculative bubble and financial crises of the late 1990s and the first decade of the twenty-first century. My overall frame is not so much "American poetry"—I begin with the British Auden and end with Davies, who is Canadian—as the "American century," because that designation foregrounds the arc of hegemony that is part of the story of the recurring crises of the period. The book moves in roughly chronological fashion, though I take the strong influence of Auden on Ashbery as permission to move from Auden's 1940s to Ashbery's 1970s before jumping back a bit, at the beginning of Chapter 3, to Spicer's writing of the late 1950s and early 1960s.

Despite the wide, even sprawling array of poetry that one might canvas in a book on poetry and capitalism, I decided to cluster a group of poets who share influence and affinity across the twentieth century, because the amplification, revisions, and discoveries that grow out of such affinity—their family resemblances and their divergences—give a stronger picture of a multi-authored literary "matter" than a sheerly topical inventory would have. In particular I hope the chapters, in their succession, will give the reader a cumulative sense of the close relationship between the experience of crisis and the imagination of different roles of poetic textuality in addressing it.

In Chapter 1, I argue that the political and economic upheavals of the period from 1917 to 1939 defined the long careers of Ezra Pound and W. H. Auden, and that taken together, Pound and Auden bequeathed to the later poets in this study a method and a tonal practice that remain at the center of experimental poetry to this day. As Eric Hobsbawm has demonstrated, the violence of World War I and the global economic chaos of the Great Depression established the vulnerability both of representative democracy and of capitalism, without providing an immediate sense of the alternatives. For Pound, famously, this meant turning to figures of statist and corporatist authority, and a populist anticapitalism that moved rightward across his career; for Auden, it meant a passionate socialism that modulated, later in life, to a kind of Left Augustinianism that emphasized inevitable human error and its forgiveness. Poetically speaking, Pound responded to the crisis with an editorial-compositional technique of compilation and collage that meant to highlight the pedagogical role of the poet in maintaining otherwise wildly fluctuating literary and monetary value—a technique that survived the shifts in his political and economic thinking, and that proved amenable to later poets of very different bents. Auden, meanwhile, maintained across the divide of his supposed abandonment of politics for religion a consistent poetic focus on the vulnerability, even the obliterability, of human life, which expressed itself poetically in a bid for error as the link between human ontogeny and phylogeny, between wayward individuals and uncontrollable systems. These two poetic emphases—on the importance of poetry as stabilizing editorial arrangement, and on poetry as the medium for registering obliterable life—form the parameters of "the matter of capital" for the rest of the century.

In Chapter 2 I turn to Ashbery's poems from the 1970s, reading them against the grain of his notoriously oblique relation to public events or identifiable history. I center my analysis on 1975's *Self-Portrait in a Convex Mirror,* which I read as a record of the transformation of New York from a city of subcultures to a global financial capital. David Harvey has argued that, like Chile in 1973, New York City in the early 1970s was a laboratory for economic and political experiments that we now recognize as the techniques of neoliberal globalization—the breaking of labor, the financialization of pensions, the making private of previous public resources—and Ashbery's poems from the seventies are acutely sensitive to the effects such techniques have on aesthetic experience. And he reads them globally as well as locally: written at the uneasy tail end of the post–World War II Pax Americana, *Self-Portrait* is an elaborate staging of the guilty conscience of the global hegemon, whose subjects are both supersaturated with images and commodities and at pains to keep offstage the violence that sustains their flow. To resolve this contradiction between feeling party to hegemonic power and having no influence on it, Ashbery develops a poetics of minority, reflected both in his career-long devotion to what he calls "The Other Tradition" of eccentric, uncanonizable poets as models for his own work, and in *Self-Portrait*'s recurring figures of what I call "optional apocalypse"—looming disaster that the poet believes he can simply choose to "wander away" from. This insistent minority, I argue, does not so much fit the received narrative of Ashbery's (and so-called "postmodern" poetry's) abandonment of the Audenian first-person poetic subject, as it suggests a kind of protection for it, a stashing away of poetic personhood that represents a guilty, unstable, and covert alignment of the hapless subject of the hegemon with other wanderers and vagrants, whom Ashbery locates elsewhere, "on the other side of the mountains."

Chapter 3 explores how, on the West Coast, two generations of poets took up the Poundian technique of compendium and collage and turned it to different ends. In the late 1950s and early 1960s, the circle of San Francisco poets around Jack Spicer pursued what they called the "serial poem," in which no single lyric was meant to bear the weight of poetic force because each poem was part of a serially realized—and perhaps unrealizable—poetic "whole," with no one author. In the Spicer circle, this technique served as an integument linking younger and older writers in Spicer's San Francisco scene, where both playful collaboration and cruel tests of loyalty helped create a sense of the poetic scene as a kind of counterenclosure against the encroachments of mass culture and the terrors of the Cold War.

Spicer's serial poem also depended on his apprentice work in the Department of Linguistics at the University of California, Berkeley, where he developed a sense of poetry not so much as a freestanding aesthetic object but as an event in a "language" made up of different parts and levels—graphemes, morphemes, phonemes, sentences. The sentence was a particularly important category for Spicer, who rarely wrote in verse lines. Spicer's analogy of poetry to a linguistic sense of language, though, depended less on the technical terms themselves than on a sense that poetic pleasure could be generated out of the rapid movement among sentences and the energy embedded in the interstices between them. In this way Spicer inaugurates a shift in the Poundian technique of compilation by turning from the exemplary value of what is compiled (anecdotes about wise leaders, as in *The Cantos*) to what he saw as the uncapturable value stashed in an ever-swifter movement among literary parts (sentences, phrases).

In the 1970s and 1980s, the young poets who would come to form the movement known as Language Poetry took up Spicer's linguistic analogy, and his attention to the sentence rather than the line, and began to develop poetic techniques designed to keep pace with a surfeit of commodity and image production unknown even to Spicer. Focusing on what Ron Silliman called the "New Sentence"—not so much individual sentences as their combinatorial possibilities for paragraphs or even longer texts—the Language writers produced a torrent of work whose baffling part-whole relationships were designed to pose the question, as Barrett Watten put it, "Are we in a dire situation or do we have a relatively comfortable life?" By the late 1980s the unanswerability of this question had led the poet Michael Palmer to develop a late-Shelleyan prophetic mode in which indiscernible forms of writing stare back at us from beyond the borders of the hegemon, as if waiting for their fulfillment in frightening or liberating social formations we cannot see.

In Chapter 4, my final chapter, I use the phrase "late-late capitalism" to measure something of the catastrophic character of the current phase shift that global capital is undergoing, both extensively, through globalization, and intensively, through the colonization of political hopes and affective survival; I also use it to track the slightly camp attitude that creeps into poetic attempts to measure the approach to end-times when the idea of end-times seems itself outmoded. The chapter is set against the backdrop of the financial crisis of the first decade of the twenty-first century and focuses two books of poems, Claudia Rankine's *Don't Let Me Be Lonely* (2004) and Kevin Davies' *The Golden Age of Paraphernalia* (2008). Though they are very different books, both of them struggle to develop a kind of poetry that references its textual character as a defense against capitalist spectacle. Rankine's book, which is subtitled *An American Lyric,* brings mass-cultural material—especially the record of what Rankine sees on television during the Bush II years—alongside intimate reflections on her depressive state. Rankine also assembles, after the fashion of a scrapbook, a network of citations to European literary modernism alongside an American history of violence against black people. The book is explicitly set in the moment of transition between the dot-com 1990s and the age of the second Iraq war, and its scrapbook technique maps out a survival strategy for those years: to pit the vulnerability of textual assemblage against the mercilessness of the image stream of the first decade of the twenty-first century.

The precarious craft labor of Rankine's book finds a wage-work cousin in Davies' poems, which imagine a fascinating blend of postcatastrophic monasticism and contemporary network as the medium through which text might gather powers to survive a cataclysmic turn of the century. *The Golden Age of Paraphernalia* develops a powerful strategy of "Lateral Argument" (the title of one of the poems) in order to mimic and keep pace with what Davies sees as the colonization of matter itself by capital—indeed, the book is obsessed with whether capital in fact *produces* matter, whose humane arrangement may be out of reach by the monastic networker. The book's five poems interrupt each other, sometime occupying space on the same page, sometimes disappearing for pages at a time, giving the sense that only a wider, more fully lateralized textual space could actually make them copresent; and Davies' words, phrases, and lines are meticulously spaced, italicized, and set in small capitals, as well as subdivided by the archetypical section markers of the digital age: the vertical slash (|) and the bullet-point (•). The poetic texture created by these strategies is darker than Rankine's: laterality and subdivision, for Davies, make of poetry a kind of textual labor that does not so much keep open a space of shared vulnerability as allow the reader to peer with the poet into a digital Inferno.

This book came to completion having led me to discoveries a bit different from those I'd hoped to make. I thought I was going to write about the array of attitudes toward apocalypse and messianism in twentieth-century poetry in English; I didn't expect to focus so much on the textual imaginary of that poetry, or to find that the "dream life" of textuality (to borrow a phrase of Joshua Clover's) was so important a resource for poets trying to address the "matter of capital." Having written this book instead of the one I'd set out to write, though, I still hope to contribute to a conversation about the poetry of the last century in a few ways that I hope are fresh. I would like to think my attention to "matter" in the sense I've outlined here will allow readers of poetry to rethink a form/content divide, and see the "subject matter" of poetry as not only thematic but intertextual. At the same time, I hope I will have demonstrated that it's possible to do "thematic" readings of poems that are not merely prehensile in relation to criticism or "theory." And I hope to have at least suggested to my friends on the academic and poetic left that it is not only the poetries of witness and documentation, or movement poetries, that are worrying over the destiny that capitalism is forcing us toward. Whether I've managed any of this is of course a question for my readers to decide; my wish for all of us is to work out a reading practice for the poetry of the last century adequate to greet the new one, because the best poetry the new century has produced, so far, clearly demands it.

— 1 —
A Method and a Tone: Pound, Auden, and the Legacy of the Interwar Years

Sometime in 1946 a group of young Berkeley poets led by Jack Spicer and Robert Duncan wrote "A Canto for Ezra Pound," which they mailed to the poet, then just beginning his twelve-year incarceration at St. Elizabeth's Hospital in Washington, D.C. Duncan was 27 at the time; Spicer was 21. The collaborative poem offers a fascinating glimpse into the state of literary canon formation on the West Coast in the 1940s, and opens a window onto how Pound's poetic techniques were being absorbed by young U.S. poets at midcentury. It is written in the style of Pound's *Cantos,* and never shifts to parody, though the Duncan-Spicer group gains comic energy by replacing Pound's world-historical concerns with those shaping the lives of university students. It is a precocious, able imitation.

For my purposes, though, the poem is most interesting for two other reasons. First, it makes an emphatic distinction between gratitude for the innovation of Pound's style and technique and rejection of the uses to which the older poet had put it. And second, the poem pits Pound against another major figure for young poets of the 1940s, W. H. Auden. Here are the relevant passages:

> And Pound, avid for public virtue,
> twenty years of poetry shot thru with Econ 1A,
> twenty years in advance of the academies,
>   Thank God, it didn't work.
> With public virtue builded no man a house of good stone,
> nor was poem written to correct polity
> poem of good stone. Still, beauty
> shows thru.

Food for a generation of poets.
  1946.
Ten years after Auden's invasion.
70 odd Cantos curiously right,
curiously wrong. The cost of too much concern
for the Public Good.
. . . .
Anybody can do it.
Write like Pound, that is.
But cld. yu write it that way before Pound?
. . . .
1946. And still no Cantos in 20th Century Literature.
(NOTE: still Willa Cather, and the poems of Auden now.)
"The Cantos are too difficult. Maybe *you*" (with a sneer)
"Know what they're all about."
. . . .
If we could find a nationality, something to love
other than persons.
. . . .
MODERN POETS CAN WRITE UNDER WATER

("A Canto for Ezra Pound")

In these passages the young poets use Pound's own means to critique and celebrate him—distancing themselves from the impulse to "public virtue," the impulse to use poetry to "correct polity," but insisting that "beauty/ shows thru," and—more than that—instancing the beauty they see through the loyalty of their imitation. At every level—from the abbreviations and distortions of orthography like "cld. yu," to the reflexive construction of the poem as annotation to itself (the repeated use of "1946," and the "NOTE" on what's being taught in literature classes at Berkeley)—at every level, Spicer, Duncan, and their friends are staging their commitment to "writ[ing] like Pound." It's easy, they argue—"Anybody can do it"—but unprecedented, too: "cld. yu write that way before Pound?" Eschewing an important aspect of the content of the Cantos—its economic theorizing, and its authoritarian bent—they defend him against what they take to be the ignorance and arrogance of the academy, which Pound moved "twenty years in advance" of, and whose representatives "sneer" at the interpretive capacities of exactly those young people who understand the Cantos best.

This is not to say that Spicer and Duncan were anti-intellectual: they were both extremely learned, if hostile to the means of the academy that had nourished them. Nor were they apolitical: both Duncan and Spicer were active in very early, and risky, forms of gay politics in the Bay Area. But they did not experience "polity" as something seen from above, to be "corrected" by the kind of authoritarian leadership Pound came to admire in figures like Mussolini. They were more invested in grassroots organizing among people—gay people—who had not yet formed a social movement, and whose activities therefore were extremely tentative, if quite brave.[1] Poetically speaking, they were in a similar situation: they experienced themselves, despite their excitement with a challenging and still underappreciated modernism, as not yet part of something, a movement, a project, that would give them the chance to take the Poundian techniques they'd learned and put them to fresh use. As the closing strophe of the poem puts it: "If we could find a nationality, something to love / other than persons."

This language of nationality also appears, it's worth noting, in the poem's first mention of Auden, whose arrival on American shores is described as an "invasion." The young poets seem to be referring to his recent ubiquity on syllabi ("still Willa Cather, and the poems of Auden now") and hint that they have no truck with Auden's work. But lines in the poem, here and there, suggest an affinity with Auden's cutting sense of humor:

> 1946. "Looks as bad as any other year."
> Even an Atom bomb can't cheer it up.

They also imitate Auden's casual elevation of language, even as they are describing their affinity with Pound:

> And so I sit down among facetious voices,
> one voice determined for the moment by some
> sentimental reverence,
> reverence that makes irreverence the only Speech proper.

Implicit in passages like these is an attention to Auden that belies the young poets' dismissal of him as too easily accepted by the academy. And, indeed, Spicer's biographers have shown that Spicer and his circle picked up on Auden's enthusiasms, devouring Tolkien's *The Lord of the Rings* after hearing that Auden recommended it, and that Spicer, in particular, was eager enough for Auden's approval that he included him on a list of writers to whom he wished to have copies of his first book sent (Killian and Ellingham 122). It is also very likely that, as an identifiably gay writer in a time when taking on such an identity was rare and costly, Auden was not quite dismissible by the younger gay poets, so explicitly in need of "a nation." So it is interesting to note that, absent "persons" who would adequately make up such a nation, the Spicer and Duncan group declare their affinity, their "nationhood," through a one-line manifesto, not about poetic lineage, but about poetic medium: "MODERN POETS CAN WRITE UNDER WATER."

"Writing under water" can be a figure for writing under difficult, isolating conditions, or it can be a figure for modernism's technical reach—"modern poets" can *even* write under water. Either way, it disavows exactly what made both Auden and Pound difficult to claim directly: a direct link between politics and subject matter. A key subject for both poets, especially in the 1920s and 1930s, was capitalism and its workings; and in both cases, the attempt to think through capital in the medium of poetry had caused critical trouble. When the Spicer-Duncan group exasperatedly describe "twenty years of poetry shot thru with Econ 1A," they are echoing a general dismay with Pound's pedantry that had already been summed up by Gertrude Stein in 1933: "He was a village explainer, excellent if you were a village, but if you were not, not" (Stein 200). Auden, meanwhile, had come under attack by the end of the 1930s from across the literary-political spectrum for what critics took to be the adolescent nature of his socialism—dismissed by the Marxist critic Christopher Caudwell for advocacy of "the revolution as a kind of giant explosion which will blow up everything [Auden and his kind] feel to be hampering them," and mourned by the Catholic journal *The Tablet* as part of a generation whose "uncritical acceptance of all the revolutionary slogans of its time . . . led to the waste and destruction of its immense abilities" (quoted in Smith 4–6). By midcentury both poets were looking back on their earlier work with regret, Pound plunging into depression and reportedly bemoaning the anti-Semitism he'd allowed to factor into his economic thinking, and Auden excising leftist manifestos like "Spain" and internationalist pleas like "September 1, 1939" from collections of his poetry.[2] For younger poets, this led to a deep instability in how to read the work of both writers: was Pound a rebel or a curmudgeon? Was Auden a heroic idealist or a pampered naïf?

There is a story to be told about how two such central literary figures could come to question their own work so deeply, and, further, about the ambivalent and complex claims to these writers' legacies that younger writers would make from midcentury on. Clearly, after the 1930s, mixing economics and poetry was seen as a recipe for aesthetic disaster. But the impression of disaster comes as much from political developments after the 1930s as it does from any failure of the poets themselves. It is hard to underestimate the degree to which the victory of the United States and its allies in World War II reshaped the ideological landscape of the 1940s and 1950s, making it easy, for instance, to dismiss collectivist aspirations on the left as no different from the mass politics of totalitarian regimes. This linking of communism and totalitarianism, or communism and fascism, as equivalent forms of mass politics, had tremendous discursive power, perhaps because it drew on an overlap between conservative anticommunism and liberal opposition to Stalinism.[3] The rhetorical effects of this ideological shift to the right were manifold, of course, and extended far beyond the very specific story I want to tell here; but we can say, returning to the question of the later reception of Auden and Pound in the United States, that this shift made any attempt by poets to write critically about capitalism—from the left or the right—seem in retrospect hysterical, adolescent, or curmudgeonly.

Unfortunately, the other major option for poets trying to think through capitalism after Auden and Pound presented its own problems. A wide range of historians of politics, economics, culture, and literature have demonstrated that U.S. cultural hegemony after World War II depended on a close link between political liberalism and consumer-driven capitalism, so that expressions of individuality tended to be routed through the medium of the market, as forms of choice among commodities.[4] It was not difficult for contemporary observers to find this link a hollow one—indeed, many popular and mass-cultural forms reflected on it, even as they participated in it—but it was difficult, given the demolition of leftist alternatives, to ground aesthetic experience in anything else. This complex dynamic undoubtedly factors into the Spicer-Duncan group's thinking when they write that they are seeking "something to love / other than persons."

But the subject matter—the relation to "persons" to capitalism—would not go away, even if it was cartooned as "Econ 1A": the postwar victories of capitalism and its liberal political framework made it an inevitable object of poetic attention. So how should younger poets write about it, without recourse to Pound's authoritarian populism, or Auden's early championing of poetic solidarity with an international working class, or a hollow triumphalism that masked the endless pursuit of commodities with the language of the dignity of the individual? Unfortunately the short answer to that question is contradictory: despite everything, younger poets turned to writers like Pound and Auden anyway. As for why they did, and what it was in Pound and Auden that remained of use, we need to look back to the era of crisis that shaped them both.

There is a broad consensus among historians of the period between the two world wars that the 1920s and 1930s were periods of crisis, not only for relations among European nations, but for global capitalism as well. The links between the political and the economic aspects of the crisis of the interwar years are manifold, of course, and extend far beyond the scope of this study; but I would like to suggest, briefly, something of the way these two aspects of the crisis registered at the level of personhood, both collective and individual.

In the aftermath of the First World War, which itself had extended military violence further than ever before into civilian life, the status of the person as the subject of political representation and as the agent of economic activity became more entwined, but also more pressurized. The economic devastation of Europe bred political crisis throughout the region, which expressed itself not only in massive labor unrest but also in the repeated liquidation of legislative bodies in the period: indeed, "liquidation" describes both the tension between heads of state and representative bodies, on the one hand, and the aims of a very stark class war, on the other. Eric Hobsbawm points out that at least seventeen legislative bodies across the continent were dissolved between 1918 and 1939; and Michel Beaud, in his history of global capitalism, cites U.S. Treasury Secretary Andrew W. Mellon's declaration that the solution to the productive, financial, and labor aspects of the economic crisis was to "liquidate labor, liquidate stocks, liquidate the farmers" (Hobsbawm 111).[5] This language owes much to the experience of "total war" in 1914–1918, which, as Hobsbawm notes, had not only military victory but complete annihilation of the enemy as its aim: Beaud cites not only U.S. officials referring to trade policy as "the other war, the economic war," but public discourse on labor policy as well, including a *London Times* article denouncing the British rail strikes of 1919 by writing that "as was the war with Germany, this must be a war to the end" (Hobsbawm 49–55; Beaud 170, 187). Conflicts between states and struggles between classes were both rendered in absolute terms.

This absolute language is belied, though, by interwar developments that would eventually provide economic security to the United States and Western Europe after the Second World War. In the 1920s and 1930s, democratic and fascist states alike began to experiment with massive governmental intervention into the economy, facilitating public works and acting, as Harry Shutt puts its, as "lender of last resort" for private economic activity. These early forms of Keynesianism, predating the Bretton Woods system of global economic regulation, were designed both to "prime the pump" of entrepreneurial activity and to forestall massive labor revolts by creating employment regardless of downturns in the business cycle. Though these employment stabilization programs, and the new forms of social security that accompanied them, were not enough to prevent the onset of another world war, they laid the groundwork for a postwar system in Europe and the United States that depended, not only on a stricter regulatory environment for the movement of capital, but also on the buying power of wage-earning classes. The Bretton Woods system is generally understood as having stabilized the global economy after World War II by virtue of the stricter controls it placed on speculation and investment; but it is also the case that the expansion of consumption of non-necessities to the working classes also gave outlets for the increased productive capacities of capital in the early and mid-twentieth century. Observers had noted as early as the late nineteenth century that the markets for cheap consumables softened the blow of the long depression that began in 1873; and by the mid-twentieth century, this incidental development had been seized on as one key to modulating the ups and downs of the business cycle (Shutt 10–11). This active cultivation of a consumer class, and the work of expanding it downward, had not yet become central in the interwar years, but it was already in play.

So the era that Hobsbawm calls "The Age of Catastrophe" raised the specter of the sheer obliterability of human life; put in question the viability of representative democracy, along with its corollary forms of political enfranchisement; and began, if unsystematically, to link the stability of the world economy to an ever-expanding, and ever-intensifying, process of consumption that linked political personhood to commodity activity.

As long as there were enough people able to continue to buy non-necessities, it came to seem, the political structures of representative government could remain untroubled and the possibility of mass violence kept at bay. That this interwar conjunction of the political and economic problems and strategies was specifically capitalist is made clear by reactions to the emergence, after 1917, of a noncapitalist world centered on Soviet Russia, whose seeming immunity to the ups and downs of the business cycle in the 1920s and 1930s led both to strident anticommunism and to social-democratic compromises between labor and capital in the United States and Europe alike.[6]

I visit these very disparate, and very large-scale, political and economic developments because I think they establish the coordinates for the concerns that Pound and Auden—both very large-scale thinkers—struggled with throughout their long careers. Needless to say, the two poets responded very differently to the crises of the 1920s and 1930s; but I want to suggest, in the rest of this chapter, that the problems posed by those crises remained at the center of both writers' poetry throughout their careers. I will also suggest that the poetics Pound and Auden developed in response to the crises of the interwar years form the two poles between which the later poets in this study have moved as they try to keep pace with, and offer alternatives to, the forms of personhood and aesthetic experience that emerge from twentieth-century capitalism.

The troubled links between poetry and economics in Pound's work are a central subject of the scholarship on him; the quality and breadth of this scholarship is considerable.[7] The aim of my attention to Pound is to highlight a particular link between Pound's economic thinking and the technique he perfected for writing *The Cantos*. First, though, it is probably worth noting the depth and persistence of Pound's concern with "economy" across his career, and how primally Pound experienced it. Critics such as Richard Siebruth and Maud Ellman have noted the sexual valences attached to the idea of usury in Pound, not least the way he links it to sodomy; and Pound's biographers have recorded the poet's reflections on childhood visits to the mint in Philadelphia, where his father worked. The task of determining the quality of silver, for instance—part of his father's job—seemed to the young poet the work "of a master alchemist in a Greek temple," and it is linked, in Pound's memory, to the image of the manual laborers, stripped to the waist, shoveling silver coins in the heat of the mint (Crunden 85).

Contrast this manly labor of physical contact with the source of value, and expert discernment of its integrity, with Pound's "Portrait D'Une Femme" of 1912, in which the 27-year-old poet dismisses a wealthy London woman for the way her mind has come to resemble a useless cabinet of curiosities. The poem begins:

> Your mind and you are our Sargasso Sea,
> London has swept about you this score years
> And bright ships left you this or that in fee:
> Ideas, old gossip, oddments of all things,
> Strange spars of knowledge and dimmed wares of price.
>
> (*Personae*, 57)

The poet deftly combines images of stasis (the seaweed-clogged sea), idleness ("gossip"), uselessness ("oddments"), and outmodedness ("dimmed wares of price") to sketch his "portrait" of this woman's mental life, whose analogy to the traffic in non-useful items is so sustained as to surpass analogy and become contiguous with the unrealized value and clogged circulation of the objects themselves, which accumulate into a "hoard" until they signify, at the poem's conclusion, her dispossession and her alienation:

> You are a person of some interest, one comes to you
> And takes strange gain away:
> Trophies fished up; some curious suggestion;
> Fact that leads nowhere; and a tale for two,
> Pregnant with mandrakes, or with something else
> That might prove useful and yet never proves,
> That never fits a corner or shows use,
> Or finds its hour upon the loom of days:
> The tarnished, gaudy, wonderful old work;
> Idols and ambergris and rare inlays,
> These are your riches, your great store; and yet
> For all this sea-hoard of deciduous things,
> Strange woods half sodden, and new brighter stuff:
> In the slow float of differing light and deep,
> No! there is nothing! In the whole and all,
> Nothing that's quite your own.
> Yet this is you.

I find this poem fascinating in relation to the Pound corpus. In its economic language (not just the "wares of price," but "interest," "gain," "useful," and "use"; "work," "riches," "store," and "hoard"), the poem previews the framework by which Pound will later contrast usefulness and the consumption of necessities to hoarding and usury, but there is a fondness for the poem's subject that disappears in the later work—a wistfulness, almost. It registers formally in the Browning-esque rhyme scheme and the lining up of appositive phrases, which allow for a rhetorical accumulation not entirely at odds with the woman's twenty years of gossip and chatter in London. I have always wished I could hear the young Pound reading this poem as clearly as we can hear the furious, vatic readings of Canto XLV.

The poem can also serve, should we want it to, as a poetic rendition of one ungenerous reading of *The Cantos,* from which so many readers have "taken strange gain away," traversing "fact that leads nowhere" to produce a "whole" that does not quite signify. Put more generously, the lost gentleness and the historical irony we can now read into "Portrait D'Une Femme" make it easier for me, at least, to measure the terror and the pathos that emerge in *The Cantos*—when the economics of the poems is depersonalized and systemic, and the rhetoric is built out of juxtapositions rather than continuities.

I'd like to turn now to one expression of that economics, and muse a bit on its rhetorical forms. I've included, below, a relatively continuous, appositive passage from Canto XXXVIII, composed in 1933. The passage glosses the Social Credit theory of Clifford Hugh Douglas, whose underconsumptionist economics seized hold of Pound's imagination in the early 1930s and became the framework for his economic thinking for the rest of his life. The passage quite succinctly gives a picture of the basics of Douglas's theory:

> A factory
> has also another aspect, which we call the financial aspect
> It gives people the power to buy (wages, dividends
> which are power to buy) but it is also the cause of prices
> or values, financial, I mean financial values
> It pays workers, it pays *for* material.
> What it pays in wages and dividends
> stays fluid, as power to buy, and this power is less,

per forza, damn blast your intellex, is less
than the total payments made by the factory
(as wages, dividends, AND payments for raw material
bank charges, etcetera)
and all, that is the whole, that is the total,
of these is added to the total of prices
caused by that factory, any damn factory,
and there is and must be therefore a clog
and the power to purchase can never
(under the present system) catch up with
prices at large,
  and the light became so bright and so blindin'
in this layer of paradise
  that the mind of man was bewildered.

(190)

This passage has almost none of the adventuresome textual overlay that is the great technical advance of *The Cantos;* probably for the sake of pedagogy, it wends its way across 22 lines in a single voice and mostly one language, dipping only briefly into Italian ("per forza"), and marking its asides with polite parentheses. Even the leap across white space to Dante's *Paradiso* ("so blindin'") lands in a colloquial English. This is perhaps because Douglas's theory demands straightforward explication: literally known as an "A + B theorem," it tries to grasp the scarcity of goods in economic hard times by pointing out that the amount of money paid to produce goods in industrial capitalism is less than the amount the workers take home in wages. The theorem would be rendered

$$A + B = P$$
$$A < P$$

where wages, salaries, and dividends (A) are less than the aggregate price of goods (P), because of the bank charges, royalties, and taxes (B) by which the financial sector funds the industrial sector—or, put in the terms of the theory, the fees by which the financial sector profits off of the industrial sector.

As Leon Surette puts it, the rhetoric of Canto XXXVIII "reflects the frustration of a man unable to convince others of the truth of a self-evident observation" (29). And Pound does write here as if he is baffled by the inability of his imagined listeners to understand a theory so straightforward as Douglas's: "damn blast your intellex." For some reason, Pound seems vexed to find, Douglas's surpassingly simple formula causes bewilderment when it should bring illumination. This may be because the formula's simplicity comes at a cost: as Surette points out, "It is entirely inadequate to categorize aggregate transactions as either revenues or disbursements, since every disbursement is a revenue for some other economic agent, and vice versa" (30). In other words, Douglas's theory, while trying to explain why workers can't afford to buy the very goods they produce, skips over the question of relations of production in its race to summarize economic activity. The "light" of the theory is "so bright and so blindin'," then, not only because it summarizes a very complex system, but because the system's complexity "blasts" through the theory's summarization. The theory gives a glimpse, you might say, of the totality of economic relations, and the glimpse overwhelms the theory, leaving its audience blind and its expositor baffled by the blindness.

This irony gets us to the crux of Pound's legacy for writers like Spicer and Duncan, who were so grateful for his technical innovations but so impatient with his "Econ 1A": there is a pedagogical impulse driving *The Cantos*, and while their famous *paideuma* leads Pound to techniques of compression that remain generative for younger poets eighty years later, that pedagogy threatens at every turn to overwhelm the poem. As Michael André Bernstein puts it, *The Cantos* began by seeking readers but ended up requiring students. He also argues that it is only because Pound failed to achieve his aim for the poem—to find a master code that would unify his disparate materials—that later poets could appreciate his methods of compression and juxtaposition, because they did not finally seal themselves off into mere pedagogy (145).[8]

I would like to think through the implications of this irony in the legacy of Pound, by which his techniques' local excitement and ultimate failure (at least by the measure of Pound's ambitions) get taken up later in the century, under different economic and political conditions than the ones that led Pound down his particular road. To do this, I think we need to look to the dynamics of poetic economy in Pound, and to the pressure point where "poetry" and "economy" diverge.

We know that both the commodity culture of the early twentieth century and the economic crisis of the Great Depression led Pound to attempt the development of a poetic method that would open his readers' eyes to the truth of a system gone awry. Pound's adherence to Douglas's underconsumption theory is the most explicit economic expression of this will to explain systemic problems in the media of poetry and literary prose, but during the Depression it led Pound not only to explicatory passages like the "factory" passage from Canto XXXVIII, above, but also to write an *ABC of Economics* (also 1933), which meanders and excoriates in equal measure, and which is arguably less effective than the economics in *The Cantos* at getting Pound's theories across.

The explicatory text from this period that has proven more lasting, of course, is 1934's *ABC of Reading,* which sets out not only a syllabus for its readers but a technique for reading texts. This technique is famously "economic," not least because it is driven by numbers at every level, from the single poem, to anthologies of poems, even to the general category "poetry." In one "Exercise" Pound writes, "Let the student try to decide if whether there are 100 good poems in whatever general anthology he possesses; or fifty, or thirty" (143–145).

He advises the same technique for understanding the value embedded in individual poems:

> How many of the poems [the student] first thinks of will be poems having one good line, or two or three lines that stick in the memory, but which he will have great difficulty in reading to the end, or from which he can remember nothing save the pleasing line?

And he concludes by encouraging the application of this discernment at the level of the poetic, in general:

> Let the student hunt for a dozen poems that are different from any of the exhibits, or that introduce some new component, or enlarge his conception of poetry, by bringing in some kind of matter, or mode of expression not yet touched on.

The pleasure in reading this advice, even today, is in Pound's readiness to disaggregate the "units" of literature into components one level down: breaking anthologies into poems, poems into lines, and lines (in other exercises) into words. This mutates effortlessly into the possibility of the "enlargement" of the student's "conception of poetry," its openness to the new, which—momentarily, at least—Pound trusts his students to discern. Indeed, in the exercises from *ABC of Reading,* the obvious dangers of so quantitatively driven a notion of literary economy are staved off by the sense—Pound's, but also the reader's—that Pound is opening up the field of the literary by breaking it down into parts to be reassembled in a superior, or more pleasing, form.

The holistic sense of poetry in *ABC of Reading* begins as an explicit humanism. In an early essay collected in *Pavannes and Divisions* as "Notes on Elizabethan Classicists," Pound writes with resentment that in traditional grammatical education "the [classical] poets are made an exercise, a means of teaching the language" (204).[9] By "exercise," here, Pound means not his own exercises of breaking down poetries in order to find the good parts, but the abjuring of questions of value that grounded his generation's classical education—what he calls "the uncritical scholarly attitude" in which reverence for Greek and Latin obscures differences in quality between good or bad Greek and Latin poems. Against this scholarly attitude, Pound writes, "the classics should be humanly, rather than philologically, taught." And this humanism depends on breadth: "The humanizing influence of the classics depends more on a wide knowledge, a reading knowledge, than on an ability to write exercises in Latin" (205–207).

In 1918 Pound's criticism of classical teaching centers on this "uncritical scholarly attitude," its conservatism, and its pomposity (he calls it "fustian"). By 1933, however, he is describing the problem with bad teaching as an economic one. Along with the quantitative protocols for winnowing poetry down it is best parts, *ABC of Reading* contains very funny, but deadly serious, criticisms of bad teaching that center on the need for money. Like any wage worker, Pound says, teachers have to soldier a bit, to fill the time: "The lecturer," he writes, is no more than "a man who must talk for an hour," and "[His] first problem is to have enough words to fill forty or sixty minutes" (83). The same problem applies to writing for pay: one becomes distracted away from trying to say something accurate by the problem of needing to fill the page with a certain amount of words, and this creates writing that he calls "false"—probably bad writing, but, worse than that, writing that drifts from its aim and derails the purpose of writing, which is not to facilitate the movement of money but to tell the truth. Pound includes himself among the guilty, here:

> Be as honest as you like, but the danger is there even when one knows it. I have felt the chill even in this brief booklet. In pure good will, but because one must make a rough estimate, the publishers sent me a contract: 40,000 to 50,000 words. I may run over it, but it introduces a 'factor,' a component of error, a distraction from the true problem:
>
> What is the simplest possible statement? (83–84)

Self-awareness is not enough to prevent yourself from becoming a bad teacher or a bad writer: writing for pay, teaching by the minute, causes bad writing and bad pedagogy. Note, though, that even as Pound insists on the economic character of the problem of bad teaching, he sees something deeper still, a relation between "error" and simple statements—what he calls "the true problem." The "true problem," I think, is the problem of truth and error more than it is the problem of justice: in this critique of the economy, justice follows on truth, not the other way around. According to Douglas's underconsumption theory, there is no material reason for scarcity in industrial society. In a well-functioning economy, in which economic middlemen were eliminated, everyone would have enough to survive, and beyond the marginal time required for the production of necessities, no one would have to perform tasks for which they are ill-suited. Indeed, in that better society, no one should. As Pound puts it: "The chief cause of false writing is economic. Many writers need or want money. These writers could be cured by an application of bank notes" (193–194).

So Pound moves from a holistic, humanist critique of bad philological classicism to a quantitative critique of "false," soldiering teaching and writing. But this "economic" critique, hitched though it is to underconsumptionist economic theory, has humanist roots as well. And it does not displace the holistic one: Pound models both holistic and economic principles in *The Cantos,* which are not only brilliantly to the point at the level of the phrase, but combinatory in the way he advises, highlighting fragments of the best writing and the best speech from different authors and juxtaposing them so as to "enlarge" the reader's "conception of poetry." Indeed, one way to read Pound's "modernism" is as a return to principles of humanist pedagogy that also highlighted economy and juxtaposition.

I think this is the method that Pound bequeathed to younger writers in *The Cantos:* a humanist writing-as-pedagogy retooled for the twentieth century. This method stages itself immediately, at the end of Canto I:

And then Anticlea came.
Lie quiet Divus. I mean, that is, Andreas Divus,
In officina Wecheli, 1538, out of Homer.
And he sailed, by Sirens and thence outward and away
And unto Circe.

Venerandum,
In the Cretan's phrase, with the golden crown, Aphrodite,
Cypri munimenta sortita est, mirthful, orichalchi, with golden
Girdles and breast bands, thou with dark eyelids
Bearing the golden bough of Argicida. So that:

(5)

The passage describes the appearances of Tiresias and Anticlea to Odysseus in Book XI of the *Odyssey,* and it foregrounds itself as a textual citation with the famous reference to Andreas Divus, which interrupts the frame story of the Canto, and prepares readers for the abrupt "So that:" that ends the poem.

This closing passage from Canto I operates by doubling and repeating motifs from the level of the morpheme to the levels of language and civilization. The story of Odysseus raising the ghost of Tiresias is repeated in the figure of Pound resurrecting Homer through a citation of the Latin translation of Andreas Divus; and Pound's restaging of the Homeric episode in poetic lines modeled on Anglo-Saxon accentual verse makes a bid for the Cantos as capacious enough to include both northern and southern, "classical" and "barbarian" literary traditions. These repetitions, echoes, and overlays can be read as part of a modernist project of collage and startling juxtapositions, as Peter Nicholls does, when he suggests that Pound's technique is to stage a "collision of time-schemes, exploring the gap or space between two momentary perceptions" (172). They can also be interpreted as tools in a culturally synthetic project, as Andrew DuBois and Frank Lentricchia do when they read the passage as creating "an illusion of three literary traditions [Greek, Latin, and English] simultaneously present in culturally mixed traces of diction and proper names" (161). These two readings need not cancel each other out: together they suggest that Pound's interruptive strategies had a synthetic aim, that he meant to startle readers back into a sense of tradition.

These interpretations of the significance of the linguistic and civilizational overlays in Canto I (and in *The Cantos* at large) can be fleshed out in more detail if we notice the poem's scalar repetitions as well as its cross-linguistic, cross-cultural parallels. Yes, literary scenes are repeated: not only does Odysseus's sacrifice produce two revenants, one desired (Tiresias) and one unexpected (his mother, Anticlea), but Pound's calling forth the dead (Homer) and a goddess (Aphrodite) also produces the ghost of

Andreas Divus, whose translation Pound depends on, but whom he urges to "lie quiet." Words are repeated, too—the "golden" of Aphrodite's girdle and the "golden" of the bough she carries (the bough itself a triple reference to the bough given to Hermes after he slays Argus, the bough by which Aeneas gains entrance to the underworld in the *Aeneid,* and to Frazer's *The Golden Bough*). And morphological fragments repeat themselves, as well, as "Wecheli" (the sixteenth-century bookmaker) mutates into "orichalchi"—the Middle English for the copper of Aphrodite's earrings in Georgius Dartona's translation of the Second Homeric Hymn to Aphrodite (Terrell 3). These mutations should be lined up with the word repetitions, the macaronic shifts from Middle English to modern English, and to Latin inside single sentences, the troping of scenes of calling forth the dead in different poems, and the Anglo-Saxon prosody used to revisit the Greek text, not only because of the aims they suggest—a fractured textual surface designed both to startle and to provoke synthesis—but because of the techniques they exemplify.

In *ABC of Reading,* as we have seen, Pound attempts to school new readers in a sensitivity to economy at different levels of scale—training them to find the best words in lines, the best lines in poems, the best poems in anthologies, and the best material outside anthologies, so as to "enlarge" the student's "conception of poetry." The differences among these scales of textual matter are irrelevant to Pound: he believes that the same skill of economy can be applied to all of them indifferently, that what is "best" will jump out at the student in the same way whether she is looking at words, or lines, or poems, or poetry as a whole. This technique derives from the same milieu as the holism Pound extolled earlier, in "Notes on Elizabethan Classicists": it belongs to humanist rhetoric, especially the tradition of composition made popular in the Renaissance by the use of Erasmus's *de Copia* of 1512. As Richard Halpern points out, the pedagogical innovation of Erasmian rhetoric was to displace a classicist educational model that focused less on "rote memorization" than on "stylistic imitation"—in particular, a stylistic imitation built around "an image of speech" in which the student imagines himself a "familiar interlocutor" with the text, whose stylistic principles he will absorb by placing himself in dialog with it, rather than through slavish memorization of it (33–34). This account of Erasmian innovation certainly echoes descriptions of Pound's own innovations in *The Cantos*—as, for instance, when Ronald Bush notes Pound's debt to the technique Browning developed in *Sordello* of placing his character "inside a discourse," and thereby requiring fewer external markers of place, time, and character to locate the poem's speaker and his story (Genesis 76:238–239). Halpern also argues, though, that a key feature of Erasmian *copia* was the "destruction of content": that the practice of rummaging through classical authors for the choicest phrases, the most elegant arrangement of words, had the cumulative effect of neutralizing the content of the source texts. As Halpern puts it, "Reading for copia tended to decode the poetic text by atomizing its larger structures of meaning and ideological content and by resolving it into generative strategies of style . . . and dissociative bits of elocutionary material." He adds that, as the copia practice of the schools met the innovations of the printing press, a reading practice built around compendia and commonplace collections led to a Tudor rhetorical culture "of the excerpt, the ornament, and the fragment" (47, 49).

Halpern distinguishes this Erasmian pedagogy of imitation and dissociation from an earlier model of memorization that he calls "sovereign"; the Erasmian model, he suggests, is more "civic." But Pound blends the two in his own remarks on compendia in *ABC of Reading* when he praises, not only the compendium as a lean, economic form, but the rulers who supposedly made them: he cites the legend of the tyrant Peisistratus finding the Homeric corpus in disarray, and ordering it to be reconstructed correctly, and he praises an unnamed Noh emperor who decided that there were "TOO MANY NOH PLAYS" and created a slimmed-down compendium of them, thereby ensuring their survival (92). In Pound the philosopher-king is replaced by a tyrant-despot who is also a textual critic and a humanist pedagogue. The poetic technique of juxtaposition and cultural synthesis that Pound constructs as a bridge between two senses of "economy"—the "simplest possible statement" and the most efficient circulation of goods—is itself built out of the blur between two social roles, that of the sovereign and that of the scholar.

So the literary expression of Pound's economic theories is a compositional practice that depends on the assembly of fragments, the best fragments, into a textual system with strong ideological aims—the revival of the epic impulse, the synthesis of modern and classical literary achievement, the championing of strong centralized authority as the corollary and cause of literary economy. But the humanist technique Pound borrows from does not blend perfectly with these aims, partly because of its cumulative effect, which is to create textual systems that achieve a kind of self-enclosure as they gain in mass and complexity. Halpern notes that this technique, with its emphasis on style rather than content and meaning, "tended to promote eloquence at the cost of dissolving conviction," that it "tended to neutralize all received ideological content" (49–50). The gamble of this technique is that the ideological neutralization that comes from an emphasis on style rather than content will be compensated for by an ideological stabilization produced by the reader, who reconstructs the content distributed across instances of exemplary style; but this gets *The Cantos* back to the problem Bernstein describes, the problem of *The Cantos*' readers needing to become students, endlessly tracking the poem's references so as to build an intertextual content into what is present in the isolated codex primarily as technique. The two senses of "economy" that Pound wished to unite—simple statements in words, and efficient circulation of goods—await reunion; meanwhile the achievement of an "overall meaning" of the poem remains out of reach, and the technique of the poem cannot be guaranteed to produce the social form it imagines.[10]

Probably a more accurate statement of this problem would be to say that the two senses of "economy" that attracted Pound remain apart, not only because the poem's humanist technique cannot unite them, but because Pound, as a poet with a humanist-textualist bent, cannot become counsel to power as he wished: he cannot, simply by writing as a humanist, revive that part of the history of humanism in which scholars could serve as advisors to princes. His appeals to Mussolini went unheeded; his eagerness to serve as an economic advisor to Douglas was politely ignored (Surette 212). Instead he became a great poet, a brilliant editor, an original essayist, an adventuresome translator; in other words, he submitted to exactly the "error" he warned against in *ABC of Reading*: he became a writer for money. We might listen for the echo of this sense of "error" in the late appearances of the word in the Pisan Cantos, and in the final complete Canto, number CXVI—those famous "admissions of failure," where Pound in fact redoubles his self-justification:

> Here error is all in the not done,
> all in the diffidence that faltered
>
> (Canto LXXXI, 521–522)

> But the beauty is not the madness
> Tho' my errors and wrecks lie about me.

And I am not a demigod,
I cannot make it cohere.
. . .
. . . it coheres all right
        even if my notes do not cohere.
Many errors,
                a little rightness,
to excuse his hell
                        and my paradiso.

(Canto CXVI, 795–797)

There is a heroic resoluteness in these passages, as well as plain stubbornness: if *only,* they suggest—if only I had not allowed myself to become distracted from the project . . .

This sense of "error," if we listen for it, means not only Pound's understandable failure to find a master code for *The Cantos,* but the failure of poetic work to become advisorial to state power, or even to economic theory. Pound, it turned out, was as much subject to modern divisions of labor as anyone else, though everything in his technique was designed to overcome them. In Chapter 3, I will outline how later poets, taking up Pound's techniques of textual collation, compilation, and juxtaposition, will take up his method for exactly the reason it frustrated Pound. First, though, I want to turn to another body of work, W. H. Auden's, because like Pound, Auden developed an acute sense of the catastrophic wrongness of human divisions of labor during the interwar years, and like Pound he met it with a highly thought-through sense of poetry as textual, as part of a textual network—though Auden's sense of poetry's textuality ends up bequeathing to later poets, not a method, but a tone.

Auden, 21 years younger than Pound, was 11 years old when World War I ended, and 31 when the Second World War began. He traveled widely in the years between the wars, living for several months in Weimar Berlin, journeying to Iceland with Louis MacNeice to produce a travel book, visiting the front in the Spanish Civil War, and spending part of 1938 in Hong Kong with Christopher Isherwood, trying to write about the Second Sino-Japanese War. Especially in Spain and in China, the young Auden seemed to be trying to get hold of a sense of historical crisis by placing himself near its flash points—an effort of which he was later quite critical. In a 1940 review of Alvah C. Bessie's *Men in Battle: A Story of Americans in Spain,* he wrote, "Like Mr Bessie, I have known many people who went to Spain to achieve self-integration. Some are dead; but of the survivors I do not know a single one whose disease was cured by this desperate action." He includes himself in this desperate desire to seamlessly experience the world-historical and the personal, reflecting on what he takes to be his perverse excitement in the buildup to World War II:

> In the Munich crisis [when Hitler threatened to invade Czech Sudetenland] I listened to the radio with a happy excitement, secretly hoping there would be a war, a hope for which I found excellent political reasons. This September, whenever I listened to a radio I started to cry. My attitude had changed because the personal problem which in 1938 was still unsolved and which in despair I was looking to world events to solve for me, was solved this year. (*Prose,* 2:39–41)

These implicitly psychoanalytic remarks suggest that one cannot simply "self-integrate" by inserting oneself physically into the scene of political conflict, hoping to help resolve it; to do so is to misinterpret the movement of political events as merely a script for one's own "personal problems." This seems an apt critique; but it does not exhaust Auden's desire to understand what he clearly experienced as an intimate link between world events and personal integration. He comes closer to making that link when he trades psychoanalytic critique for a certain historical rhetoric. In the notes attached to his long poem "New Year Letter"—written in 1940, the same year as his *Common Sense* review—Auden includes this brief anecdote:

> X. was a Prussian banker. Ruined by the post-war inflation, he took a job as a private detective in a Berlin department store. He had not been there long before he had to arrest his own grandmother for shoplifting. (95)

Auden frames this footnote with a discussion of the idea of *arete* in Greek culture, so that the Prussian banker's submission to the historical irony of having to arrest his own grandmother was meant as an example of the destruction of self-actualization. The inflation of the German 1920s, rather than a "personal problem," provides the link between the vicissitudes of the self and the large-scale events of political (and, clearly, economic) life.

This recourse to a Greek ideal of wholeness as the measure by which to judge modern distortions of the self is not incidental to the footnote. In his introduction to Viking Press's *Portable Greek Reader* of 1948, Auden makes an ancient–modern comparison based on a rhetoric of classical integration and modern fragmentation:

> There is no Greek literary work of art as great as *The Divine Comedy*, there is no extant series of works by a single Greek literary artist as impressive as the complete plays of Shakespeare; . . . nevertheless, the bewildered comment of any fifth century Athenian upon our society from Dante's time to our own, and with increasing sharpness every decade, would surely be: 'Yes, I can see all the works of a great civilization, but why cannot I meet any civilized persons? I encounter only specialists, artists who know nothing of science, scientists who know nothing of art, philosophers who have no interest in God, priests who are unconcerned with politics, politicians who know only other politicians. (*Prose*, 2:358)

This contrast dates at least to Schiller, who makes it in terms Auden borrows entire from the sixth of Schiller's letters in *On the Aesthetic Education of Man*. For Schiller, the emphasis is on a problem of fragmentation caused by specialization; as he puts it, the difference between the ancients and the moderns is that, in modern society, "one has to go the rounds from one individual to another in order to be able to piece together a complete image of the species" (31–33).[11] The twist, in Auden, is that this ancient–modern difference is marked by systemic catastrophes like the postwar inflation in Berlin. As we will see, it is not fragmentation per se, but fragmentation as both cause and effect of systemic processes, that poses for Auden the most acute form of the problem of modern "civilization."

Like Pound, Auden responded to the crises of the interwar years by attempting to build a textual culture that is recognizably humanist—one that would be integrative and precise, able to counter the worst tendencies of inflation and violence, but also fragmentary and flexible, able to mediate between different scales of human experience. Like Pound, he understands good writing in terms of precision and the resistance to inflation: in one of the notes to "New Year Letter," he quotes Cyril Connolly saying that "the characteristic vice of the writer today is overproduction, and the major cause of overproduction is the need for money," a remark so like Pound's in *ABC of Reading* it sounds lifted from it; and in his commonplace book of 1970, *A Certain World*, the listing under "Education, Classical," reads: "it inculcates the habit, whenever one uses a word, of automatically saying, 'What is its exact meaning?'"—an echo of Pound's "What is the simplest possible statement?" (*New Year Letter,* 93; *A Certain World,* 146–147). Indeed, the form of *A Certain World* exemplifies Auden's humanist taste for compilation as wisdom, as does the eighty-page compendium of *bons mots,* case studies, and citations from experts attached to "New Year Letter." Finally, like Pound, Auden saw the activity of editing as a way for writers to mediate between this literary sense of "economy" and the "economy" that was capable of engendering such widespread crises: he edited not only Viking's *Greek Reader* and Yale's Younger Poets Series, but helped found two book clubs in the United States, The Reader's Subscription and the Mid-Century Book Club (*Prose,* 3:623). It seems clear that there was a link for Auden, as there was for Pound, between organizing the textual matter of his own writing and facilitating the development of a textual culture into which that writing could fit. Both aims were given particular focus by the economic and political trouble of the 1920s and 1930s.

Unlike Pound, however, Auden was not a monetarist, and did not set up his humanist notions of precision and flexibility, or his sense of lost *arete,* against usury or inflation per se. He was extremely wary of any attempt to reform society from the ground up, on the left or the right; it seems that his youth in the turbulent interwar period gave him an acute sense that society was structured in contradiction, not in a single uprootable mistake. Again the notes to "New Year Letter" are instructive here, written as they are at the end of the 1930s. Commenting on the difference between left and right programs for social change, he writes:

> Fascism is Socialism that has lost its faith in the future. Its slogan is Now or Never. In demanding a dictator it is really demanding the advent of the Good Life on earth through a supernatural miracle. (118)

This critique of the right-wing desire for immediate (and unmediated) change, of right-wing messianism, extends to other, more progressive forms of thought: elsewhere in the notes, he writes, "Definition of Romanticism: unawareness of the dialectic" (118). However fair or unfair this may be, it reflects a strong resistance to apocalyptic narratives of change—to which, as we will see, Auden sheepishly confesses having had an attraction.

Later, in *A Certain World,* Auden would imply that a characteristic feature of modern civilization is that the apocalypse has already happened. In an entry called "Dark Ages, Thank God for the," he cites Eric Auerbach's comparison of the styles of Ammianus and Gregory of Tours, contrasting the florid complexity of the fourth-century pagan historian and the plain, unadorned style of the sixth-century bishop. Auden's comments make a link between the *sermo humilis,* or humble manner, that Auerbach praises as the great contribution of Christendom to literary style, and the passage of a great catastrophe, the fall of Rome. For Auerbach, Ammianus' prose is beset by all the problems of a late manner, in this case a Latin "burdened by the fetters of tyrannical rules and the periodic style." In the case of Gregory's more rudimentary Latin, however,

> the catastrophe has occurred, the Empire has fallen, its organization has collapsed, the culture of antiquity has been destroyed. But the tension is over. And it is more freely and directly, no longer haunted by insoluble tasks, no longer burdened by unrealizable pretensions, that Gregory's soul faces living reality, ready to apprehend it as such and to work in it practically. (95–96)

I think this gets us to the heart of a difference between Auden and Pound, and also to the particular contribution Auden makes to the repertoire of later writers. For Pound, modernity was a form of inefficient social organization, beset by middlemen, that strong editorial compilation—within his own poems, and among them—could return to efficiency and actuality. Auden, though, conceived of modernity dialectically as a universalization of specialization that unleashed both great technical achievement and recurrent catastrophe. Rather than produce a disorienting textual surface meant to startle readers into a capacity for synthesis and reconstruction, he wanted to make poems that met universal specialization with a textual surface shot through with differences in style level. The actuality Auden cites Auerbach admiring in Gregory, the actuality by which the arrival of true catastrophe at least means "the tension is over," is a tacit permission to think about style and historical change together, not only through their relation to social station, as in classical criticism, but through historical changes to the system of station. Auden consistently conceives of these changes as catastrophic and contradictory, unleashing energies for good and for ill at once, and I think it is his great project to concoct a style to meet this historiography of contradiction.

In an elegy for Louise MacNeice that forms part of his 1963 poem "Thanksgiving for a Habitat," Auden offers this account of his lifelong friendship with MacNeice:

Friends we became by personal
  choice, but fate had already
made us neighbors. For Grammar we both inherited
  good mongrel barbarian English
which never completely succumbed to the Roman rhetoric
  or the Roman gravity, that nonsense
which stood none. Though neither of our dads, like Horace's,
  wiped his nose on his forearm,
neither was porphyry-born, and our ancestors probably
  were among those plentiful subjects
it cost less money to murder. Born so, both of us
  became self-conscious at a moment
when locomotives were named after knights in Malory,
  Science to schoolboys was known as
Stinks, and the Manor was still politically numinous:
  both watched with mixed feelings
the sack of Silence, the churches empty, the cavalry
  go, the Cosmic Model
become German, and any faith, if we had it, in immanent
  virtue died. More than ever
life-out-there is goodly, miraculous, loveable,
  but we shan't, not since Stalin and Hitler,
trust ourselves ever again: we know that, subjectively,
  all is possible.

(692)

Auden begins by doubling his Auerbachian contrast between practical Roman "nonsense" and "good mongrel barbarian English" with a contrast between "the Manor" and his and MacNeice's anonymous, disposable ancestry, implicitly lining up style and station; but these high/low juxtapositions modulate into a historical account of the poem's bivalent present, which still bears traces of both a heroic mode (trains named after knights) and a mischievous, schoolboy low style (science is "Stinks"). This bivalence deepens into contradiction in lines that depict the technical capacity by which life manages to be "More than ever / . . . goodly, miraculous, lovable," but also "more than ever" capable of mass destruction: "all is possible." The names of Stalin and Hitler, coming after the names of the knights in Malory, can be read as mutations of a residual heroic mode into an emergent systemic one: villainy become social organization.

I think Auden's desire to develop a style to meet these contradictions can explain a few long-standing observations about his poetry, especially his penchant for camp attitude, and his formal restlessness, his desire to try out as many poetic forms as he possibly could. There is a line, in Auden, that runs from Auerbachian *sermo humilis* to the strategy of camp, both "low styles" that are well-suited to signal one kind of "catastrophe" or another—the disorienting loss of a old structures of authority, or the mismatch between the transpersonal movement of a history and the embodied form of its individual actors. Even the title of the Auerbach entry in *A Certain World* signals this link, which reads like a camp rewriting of Auerbach's appreciation for the low style: "Dark Ages, Thank God for the."

Auden stages this camp effect of style discrepancy throughout his career, and it can accommodate many forms and social situations. A good early example is the pompous address in the "Address for a Prize-Day" section of his 1932 book *The Orators,* in which a returning alumnus gives to the assembled schoolboys advice that is by turns nonsensical, vacuous, and sinister; later, in the "Caliban to the Audience" section of 1944's *The Sea and the Mirror,* Auden gives Caliban the prose style of Henry James, mingling the mongrel and the aesthete in a dramatic monologue in which Caliban replaces Shakespeare as the source of information about *The Tempest.* In both cases, the campiness of the style choice is bound up with an implicit catastrophe, the replacement of authentic (or at least traditional) authority with a sorry replica. Auden's psychoanalytic bent means, of course, that he is pointing the finger at himself in these moments as much as at any actual historical process of devolution. The implication is that everyone, the poet included, lives a simulacral or debased existence when measured by the possibility of *arete,* authenticity, or wholeness. So rather than devolved authority, it might be better to say that these scenes depict the rueful comedy of the disjunct between part and whole, occupant and role, that results from the sort of nonwholeness that Auden identifies with modern specialization.

It is important that these moments are built around scenes of address, oratorical and dramatic, that have been made textual. "Address for a Prize-Day" is only one part of *The Orators,* which is framed by a series of odes, and whose complete title suggests an anthropology or sociology: *The Orators:*

An English Study. The complete title of *The Sea and the Mirror* is *The Sea and the Mirror: A Commentary on Shakespeare's The Tempest*. In both cases a camp mixture of pleasure and dismay derives from the mismatch between speaker and occasion, in a personified scene of live address. But this pleasure and dismay is met by that scene's incorporation into textuality—not in order to kill the liveness of the depicted scene, but to bring it into the fold of a textual system, to compensate for the strandedness the scenes depict by implying that they participate in something larger than themselves.

Commentary, study, commonplace book: the secondary status of the forms I've highlighted in these last pages seems strange for a poet, almost a disavowal of the traditional primacy accorded to "poetry" as a high, or intensified, or immediate literary form. For Auden, though, this secondarity is exactly poetry's saving grace—it is merely a part of what he calls, in 1937's "Letter to Lord Byron," "the total literary glory" (98).[12]

I would like to suggest in the remainder of this chapter that Auden's idea of the literary as an open-ended textual system gets us to what Auden leaves the poets, especially the American poets, who come after him. I think Auden bequeaths to these later writers exactly what they were hoping for when they expressed their wish for "something to love / other than persons." This is not because Auden is "impersonal," along the lines of an Eliot, but because he reworks an older literary model of personhood, the heroic, to meet the technically productive, but psychically fragmenting, conditions of the time. His innovation registers as a tone, most often identified as camp, but Auden's "camp" has modal and tonal cousins in the mock-heroic, in the burlesque, even—as we will see—in the elegiac. All of these modes and tones, for Auden, are linked to the *sermo humilis* that greets catastrophe; and as the Second World War approaches, they are made to bear the weight of the dialectical changes in which the subjects of the twentieth century are so helplessly caught up. This is especially true in "New Year Letter" and "In Memory of Sigmund Freud," two emblematic poems of the period, with which I will close.

"New Year Letter" was written at the very beginning of 1940, the year after Auden's arrival in New York. It could be read as a kind of cross between *The Dialectic of Enlightenment* and *Paradise Lost*. The poem addresses itself to the question of how the twentieth century can have led to the mass politics and instrumental rationality that produce the conditions for limitless destruction; and it develops an answer to this question that previews Adorno and Horkheimer's argument, four years later, that the Enlightenment promise of universal equality before a just law has developed instead into universal equivalence on the market. Technical progress, they argue—and again, Auden narrates this in the poem—produces at every moment the possibility of a kind of earthly arcadia; but it tends to bring, instead, new catastrophe, new destruction, new violence ("The Concept of Enlightenment"). In both Auden's poem and in Adorno and Horkheimer's philosophical anthropology, the engine of this dialectic between the capacity to feed and clothe everyone, and the possibility of destroying them instead, is the nexus of relations among capital, property, and exploitation—an engine for capital expansion that creates a dialectical "progress" with unexpected consequences. As Auden puts it about two-thirds of the way through the poem:

> It is the Mover who is moved.
> Whichever way we turn, we see
> Man captured by his liberty,
> The measurable take charge
> Of him who measures

The poem also has a theological angle, in which Auden tries to correlate the collective nightmare of history with individual structures of cognition and affect that lead to "sin." The devil has a role to play, as the figure who tempts the modern subject to reject Enlightenment rationality, because it has led only to the disenchantment of the world, and who tempts the leftists of the 1930s to become conservatives, because the historical forces described by Marx have led to war instead of revolution. But the theological turn in the poem is not meant to be otherworldly. At the poem's center are three unnamed heroes, easily decoded as Kant, Marx, and Darwin, who together stand in Auden's mind as prophets of human limitation, reminding modern subjects that the unleashing of their newly vast technological powers will be survivable only if those powers are matched to a sense of the contours of collective humanity that is not, despite its endless hungers, limitless. "New Year Letter" is a remarkable attempt, in the face of seemingly unnarratable complexity, to give a poetic account of that complexity's origins and consequences. If it tarries with a Miltonic idea of original sin, that "sin" is the sin of the type of abstraction that universalizes particulars into equivalence—a "sin" that is more like an error in thought, an ideology, brought about by the historical rise of the bourgeoisie.

Finally, "New Year Letter" is also a humanist document in at least two senses. First, as Michael Murphy has pointed out, both the poem's couplets and its broad survey of the capacities of humankind align it with Pope's *Essay on Man,* which itself makes use of key humanist gestures like the separation of faith and reason—"Know then thyself, presume not God to scan / The proper study of Mankind is Man"—and the location of humankind in a cosmological "middle" between the animals and the angels—"Placed on this isthmus of a middle state" (Epistle 2, lines 1–3). The middleness in which Pope situates humankind is defined by contradiction, as it is for Auden: Pope's humanity is "darkly wise, and rudely great . . . Created half to rise and half to fall." Auden will interpret these contradictions less paradoxically and more dialectically; but the humanist link to Pope is strong.[13]

Second, "New Year Letter" reads like a document of humanist textual culture for a reason I have already mentioned: appended to the forty-page poem is an eighty-one page compendium of supplementary notes, which serve to suture the poem into a network of literary and philosophical citations (especially non-English, and frequently German, in origin: Kierkegaard and Nietzsche seem central, as do Kafka, Mann, and Rilke). These notes also broaden the poem's focus to include remarks from disciplines like anthropology (Margaret Mead features prominently) and the life sciences of the day (especially midcentury biological holisms). The poem is not footnoted, per se; the poem makes perfect sense without the supplementary material, and nothing in the body of the poem indexes the supplement. But the compendium itself is back-referenced to lines in the poem. This one-way relation—notes pointing to the poem, but not the other way around—gives the relation between the two parts a slightly evidentiary feel, as though the poem were a legal argument and the notes were exhibits. Indeed, the single most frequent genre of note is a kind of casuistical fable or case study, usually implied to have been written by Auden, designed to sharpen a point made in the body of the poem.

As we will see, the poem's argument about the dialectic of progress and catastrophe, its critique of limitless and instrumental reason, and its nested situation in a compendium of citations—all these are brought into the service of developing an account of whether something like personhood can survive the twentieth century. In the elegy to MacNeice from

"Thanksgiving for a Habitat," Auden wrote about personhood for the middle classes as a recent and precarious achievement, at least from the vantage of postclassical civilization: his and MacNeice's ancestors were among those "it cost less money to murder." In that poem, he canvassed the fortunes of the proper name in the span of a few lines. In "New Year Letter," however, he devotes much more energy to the historical vicissitudes of personhood, which he investigates by moving from a present historical crisis—the coming of World War II—to its enabling conditions.

"New Year Letter" begins at a party on Long Island, where expatriates and American friends listen to music together, making "[their] minds a *civitas* of sound / Where nothing but assent was found." Meanwhile, though, "There crouch[es] the presence of The Thing"—that is, the expanding war, drawing nearer "up the staircase of events" (199). No one knows what to do to resist it, because it seems to conform no recognizable pattern:

> The situation of our time
> Surrounds us like a baffling crime.
> There lies the body half-undressed . . .
> And under lock and key the cause
> That makes a nonsense of our laws.
>
> (205)

Worse, the war seems to make a travesty of liberal and progressive political belief. In lines that echo Yeats's "Easter 1916," Auden writes:

> It lures us all: even the best,
> *Les hommes de bonne volunté,* feel
> Their politics perhaps unreal
> And all they have believed untrue,
> Are tempted to surrender to
> The grand apocalyptic dream
>
> (206)

The "apocalyptic dream," in which the war at least drives capitalism to eat itself alive, bringing about its own violent end, has roots, Auden says, in a brighter reverie, from the 1930s:

> We hoped; we waited for the day
> The State would wither clean away,
> Expecting the Millennium
> That theory promised us would come:

It didn't. Specialists must try
To detail all the reasons why;
Meanwhile at least the layman knows
That none are lost so soon as those
Who overlook their crooked nose (219)

What follows is delicate. Having proposed that it was an excess of abstraction that led to the mistaken predictions of the interwar left, Auden wrestles with the temptation to denounce abstraction: this, at least, is the role he gives to "the devil," who promises to tend to the hangover of the left:

He calls at breakfast in the role
Of blunt but sympathetic soul:
"Well, how's our Socialist this morning?"

(219)

But what the poet turns to, instead, is an attempt to historicize the baffling conditions of the present, to get at what he calls

The metaphysics of the Crowd,
The Immanent Imperative
By which the lost and injured live
In mechanised societies
Where natural intuition dies (225)

At the root of this mass causality, both immanent and mechanized, is the rise of a new human type, the bourgeois:

Over the freedom of the Will
And the right of Princes to do ill,
Emerged a new *Anthropos*, an
Empiric Economic Man
. . .
The individual let loose
To guard himself, at liberty
To starve or be forgotten

(230)

This "liberty," which masks the imperative to be "free" or die, is only graspable as the result of acts not isolable in any single person, and finally apparent in its endgame, which is war:

The average of the average man
Becomes the dead Leviathan,
Our million individual deeds,
Omissions, vanities, and creeds,
Put through the statistician's hoop
The gross behaviour of a group;
Upon each English conscience lie
Two decades of hypocrisy,
And not a German can be proud
Of what his apathy allowed

(234)

Auden argues that this outcome, so horribly more than the sum of its parts, was foreseen by the early critics of Enlightenment, whose names he capitalizes:

BLAKE shouted insults, ROUSSEAU wept,
Ironic KIERKEGAARD stared long
And muttered "All are in the wrong,"
While BAUDELAIRE went mad protesting
That progress is not interesting

(231)

This technique of capitalization is meant lightly to heroize his subjects, but also, I think, to make them memorizable, as if the readers of the poem were the imaginary schoolboys whose outline Auden so consistently sees as the outline of the human subject. Indeed, as he expands the field of those to whom the capitalized proper name matters, it comes to include the nameless who seem to have read and absorbed, probably in school, the outlines of the archetypes they long to be. These nameless figures are those to whom Enlightenment has given, not the capacity to form a just society, but only a trace relation to the heroic, a scrap of typological value affixed to persons like a gold tooth:

Each salesman now is the polite
Adventurer, the landless knight
Gawaine-Quixote . . .
An unrobust lone FISHER-KING;
Each subway face the PEQUOD of
Some ISHMAEL hunting his lost love

(239)

After close to forty pages, as the poem winds toward a conclusion, Auden runs the algorithm of this trace typology further backward, until he arrives at a scenario in which the United States, his new home, becomes legible to him as a place born as Europe was, by vast anonymous migrations. But where, for Europe, the story that grows from such migrations is the story of a "barbarian" culture encountering an emergent "Christendom" and becoming its champions, in the United States the migrations are impelled by a mixture of dreaming and working, whose emergent organizing form is a labor market and a culture industry:

> A *Völkerwanderung* occurs:
> Resourceful manufacturers
> Trek southward by progressive stages
> For sites with no floor under wages,
> No ceiling over hours; and by
> Artistic souls in small towns that lie
> Out in the weed and pollen belt
> The need for sympathy is felt,
> And east to hard New York they come;
> And self-respect drives Negroes from
> The one-crop and race-hating delta
> To northern cities helter-skelter;
> And in jalopies there migrates
> A rootless tribe from windblown states . . .
>   . . . and kids
> when their imagination bids,
> Hitch-hike a thousand miles to find
> Some Texas where real cowboys seem
> Lost in a movie-cowboy's dream.
> More even than in Europe, here
> The choice of patterns is made clear
> Which the machine imposes
>
> (237–238)

These overlapping migrations, of capitalists, of raced laboring subjects, of artists and young people, are all impelled to their movements by a market larger and more abstract than any of them, a market that gives shape to their very sense of personhood—"self-respect," "the need for sympathy," the dream of being a dreaming cowboy. This is to say that the "patterns . . . the machine imposes" are not merely secondary impositions: they have the power to create persons, to create a reality made of patterned dreams. Elsewhere in the poem, Auden writes:

All real perception, it would seem,
Has shifting contours like a dream . . .
Suppose we love, not friends or wives,
But certain patterns in our lives,
Effects that take the cause's name

(210)

In this dreamlike understanding, love grasps for patterns but vulnerably mistakes effects for causes, which is what Auden thinks "the machine" draws its power from: it latches onto a soft, phenomenologizing work of being where the desire for personhood lies, captures and organizes experience, and lures the ego with a migrating shape and the promise of a proper name.

So Auden's dialectical "essay on man" identifies a human yearning that misreads cause and effect in the name of love, a misreading he links to another mental process, the process of making things equivalent. He does not see these mental activities as innate: the yearning for a name emerges out of the vicissitudes of personhood he describes in the movement from heroes and anonymous others to universalizable but fragmentary types; and the making equivalent of every particular is a product of value creation under capital. Like Pope's "man," Auden's humanity is also wedged in a humanist middle between animality and angelhood; but for Auden, that middleness is generative, and not eternal. In placing humanity in this zone, and making it the engine of dialectical change, he has surmised a very historical unconscious.

It is this unconscious, and its relation to catastrophe, that make the tone Auden is best known for, that slightly campy tone that can slide into an irritating avuncularity, or what he called, accusing himself, "the preacher's loose immodest tone" (*New Year Letter,* 204), but that is also capable of stepping away from human particulars, seeing them as "middled," purgatorial, and finding something to love there, not in unique persons, per se, but in the attempts at personhood he finds precariously dotting the historical landscape. I don't quite mean that Auden bequeaths a clever "middle style" to later poets, though he does arguably do that; I mean that he makes the *question* of style, and its relation to the literary histories of personhood (first as station, later as fragment), the grounds on which to understand the catastrophes through which his generation lived. This is emphatically "something to love / other than persons."

One last glance at a poem, written at the beginning of World War II. "In Memory of Sigmund Freud" begins by wondering what it means to mourn a single life at the onset of mass violence:

> When there are so many we shall have to mourn,
> when grief has been made so public, and exposed
> to the critique of a whole epoch
> the frailty of our conscience and anguish,
> of whom shall we speak?
>
> (274)

The poem insists on locating Freud's greatness in the simplicity and potential universality of his investigations into the psyche, making his singularity rest on having found the right scale on which to deploy that old humanist technique, the study of poetry:

> He wasn't clever at all: he merely told
> the unhappy Present to recite the Past
> like a poetry lesson till sooner
> or later it faltered at the line where
> long ago the accusations had begun,
> and suddenly knew by whom it had been judged
>
> (274)

The technique is straightforward enough; it's the application of it to history itself, "Present" and "Past," that is quietly marked as extraordinary. And its success is measured, the poem argues, in the dissolution of Freud's personhood—not into death, but into the circulation of his ideas:

> to us he is no more a person
> but a whole climate of opinion
> under whom we conduct our different lives

Auden depicts the effect of the dispersal of Freud's personhood into the "climate" as restorative, as integrative—not only of individual personalities, instances of which he sketches in subsequent stanzas—but of the high and the low, the young and the old, of all bonds broken by a logic of punishment:

He would unite
the unequal moieties fractured
by our own well-meaning sense of justice,
would restore to the larger the wit and will
the smaller possess but can only use
for arid disputes, would give back to
the son the mother's richness of feeling

Auden does not mean Freud achieved all this; the "would" is crucial. But the subjunctive's ambition expands mightily, and movingly, at the end of the poem, which reworks the language of social station implied in the contrast between "the larger" and "the smaller" to include what he calls "the fauna of the night," the prehuman, animal impulses Freud found living in the carapace of the human. Auden sweeps them all up into a dialectic of enlightenment in which it is possible to measure history, not only from above, as it were, in the measure of the catastrophes it has produced, but from a "below" that reveals, not only human folly, but capacity, possibility. That "below" is an animal world:

he would have us remember most of all
to be enthusiastic over the night,
not only for the sense of wonder
it alone has to offer, but also
because it needs our love. With large sad eyes
its delectable creatures look up and beg
us dumbly to ask them to follow:
they are exiles who long for the future
that lies in our power, they too would rejoice
if allowed to serve enlightenment like him,
even to bear our cry of "Judas,"
as he did and all must bear who serve it.
One rational voice is dumb. Over his grave
the household of Impulse mourns one dearly loved:
sad is Eros, builder of cities,
and weeping anarchic Aphrodite.

(276)

Here the project of enlightenment is resituated in the long arc of evolutionary time, though it becomes more, not less, historical for being so: the animals' beseeching eyes, silently begging to participate in progress, make me think of a passage in Adorno's 1970 *Aesthetic Theory* on the problem of "semblance," that is, the historical vicissitudes of mimesis: "There is nothing so expressive as the eyes of animals—especially apes—which seem objectively to mourn that they are not human" (113). But most striking about this poem, I think, is how Auden's camp impulse mutates here into its cousin, a Dantean purgatorial mode in which a mix of "high" language ("sad is Eros, builder of cities") and "low" ("he wasn't clever at all") helps build a picture of cosmological middleness, the animals beneath the human, and the gods above. This middleness, along with the dispersal of the mourned Freud into a "climate of opinion," meets the demands of individual elegy in a time of mass death by proposing a shifting laterality, built out of texts, in the midst of this vertical arrangement of styles (Auden's other elegy of 1939, written for Yeats, describes the same dispersal, and like the Freud elegy calls up the figure of the "city," figure for human ambition: "Now he is scattered among a hundred cities").

In "New Year Letter" Auden urges his friends, caught up in an age of bellicose nationalism, to become with him "patriots of the now," loyal to the purgatorial muddle of a humanness still struggling to make of history something other than one long sequence of catastrophes (229). This is probably the "nation" he would have proposed to Duncan and Spicer and their friends, looking for "a nationality, something to love / other than persons." Certainly the idea of a protective scattering of personhood across a textual corpus became crucial for Spicer; but he turned more explicitly to the techniques of textual arrangement in Pound than to Auden's modal experiments in style. The stronger link to Auden in Spicer's generation is to John Ashbery.

— 2 —
John Ashbery's Optional Apocalypse

If the poetry of Auden and Pound was shaped by a crisis in global capitalism, the poems of John Ashbery, whose career maps closely onto the years of the Pax Americana, are shaped by the crises born of its victories. For the earlier poets, the crisis of capital in the interwar years made it necessary to think about which of the great ideologies, which forms of social organization, were to be championed; for Ashbery, writing in the long postwar boom, the problem is to understand the highly conditional terms of the bounty with which he finds himself surrounded.

Auden, as we saw in the last chapter, met the possibility of mass destruction by developing a dialectical understanding of style in which the humble and the vaunted mingle to produce a sense of history as dialectical, too—generative of catastrophe and ongoing promise alike. Scholarship has made clear how much the young Ashbery admired this tactic of Auden's, though he understands it in existential rather than Marxist terms. In his undergraduate thesis on Auden, Ashbery remarks that the ridiculous speeches of Caliban to the audience in *The Sea and the Mirror* solve an existential problem of authenticity: "The only solution is seeing ourselves as we are—actors in a *completely unconvincing and unbeautiful drama*" (Wasley 687). What I'd like to do in this chapter is track the transposition of this ironic, campy, purgatorial attitude, born of the interwar years, into a new historical situation.

The focus of this chapter will not be to trace continuities between Auden and Ashbery, though they are there. Rather, having established that one of Auden's achievements is the development of a dialectical understanding of style that is always in relation to catastrophe, I intend in this chapter to demonstrate that this understanding of style is something Ashbery picks up on, and that we can use it to read Ashbery historically in ways he has not been read, to date. By "style" I mean both a comportment of Ashbery's and a collection of images and ideas that assert themselves thematically across the course of his career. I am especially interested in how Ashbery's understanding of himself as a minor poet, and of poetry as a minor activity, make it possible to historicize his work, as well as to read it thematically—despite a broad critical consensus that Ashbery's work eludes thematization.[1]

There is Ashbery criticism that dissents from this view, of course, notably the criticism that pays attention to the gay "content" of his poetry. John Shoptaw's work is helpful in this regard, because Shoptaw is meticulous in his unraveling of what he calls "homotextuality"—crypt-words and blurred references to cultural and sexual specifics that Shoptaw persuasively demonstrates can be found throughout Ashbery's work *(On the Outside Looking Out).* Most helpful to me, though, has been the work of John Emil Vincent, whose extraordinarily attentive readings of Ashbery are built around a sense that it is at the level of the book, rather than the individual poem, where Ashbery makes himself most available to historically and culturally specific readings (*John Ashbery and You,* 4–5).

I have taken Vincent's cue seriously in this chapter, reading not only across the poems in his books but across his books. One yield of this reading practice, I think, is that we can begin to see Ashbery working up something like a "matter of capital" all on his own—a network of topoi that reach across the books of fifteen years and make it possible to see, even in small gestures, whole thematics being touched on (I like to think, tugged on, as in pulled threads of a tapestry). I don't have a theory of the relationship between gay content and this "matter of capital," but I hope to be able to show that there are reasons, in both cases, to argue that poetic work best thrives in a textual environment of "concealment" (Vincent, *John Ashbery and You,* 111–112). Indeed, I think it's imagining textuality as an "environment"—a "climate," Auden might have said—that allows Ashbery his tremendous leeway to assemble quite specific, quite urgent "matter" without seeming to have anything particular to say about it. For after all, who would trace its scattered elements across his many poems?

This brings us back to the main line of Ashbery criticism, the idea that he eludes thematization. Though this interpretation of Ashbery has been continuous down to the present, I'd like to pick an early and highly perceptive example, from a review by Richard Howard of 1970's *The Double Dream of Spring.* Howard writes:

> The great innovation of Ashbery's poems is that they do not explain or symbolize or even refer to some experience the poet has had, something outside themselves in the world . . . the poems are not about anything, they are something . . . For all his modesty and mildness, that is Ashbery's great symbolist assertion—that the world may exist to conclude in a book.

Howard's remarks help establish the great theme of Ashbery criticism, that his poems are about nothing, that they are textual rather than referential. In a passage just before this one, though, Howard sketches out a related way of looking at Ashbery that is a bit more suggestive for being a bit less epistemological. Ashbery's poems, he writes, are

> an active memorial to themselves, writhing in dissolute, shimmering lines without emphases or repetitions around the column their own accumulation raises . . . And if it is true that in reading poems which are habitually a gloss on their own singularity we need all the help we can get, it is also true that Ashbery wants us to enjoy our helplessness along the way. (150)

Howard's comments here strike me as especially helpful for how they link a relation to value (a self-referential "accumulation" that seems not to accumulate at all) and a relation to readers (Ashbery's "want[ing] us to enjoy our helplessness"). Together they hint at a picture of poetic minority ("mildness and modesty" . . . "singularity" . . . "helplessness") in which a quiet bid for the existential importance of textuality ("the world may end up in a book") makes it possible to enjoy some unspecified form of powerlessness.

I think it's possible to specify that powerlessness, to read it as a relationship among accumulation, textuality, and minority that is actually quite particular to the seventies—even, I'd go so far to say, to the New York City of that era. As David Harvey and others have detailed, New York in the seventies was the scene for a battle between capital and labor in which investment bankers and corporate leaders seized the opportunity of the recession of the day to unhitch the city from federal support and make it dependent on private financing. This is the crisis that led to the famous *New York Daily News* headline of October 30, 1975—"Ford to City: Drop Dead"—and that brought municipal unions into line by forcing them to invest their pensions in city bonds, thereby making the secure retirement of their members susceptible to the threat of withdrawn corporate subsidy (Harvey 44–45). The flip side of this demolition of union militancy was the concentration and spectacularization of capital exemplified in the two towers of Minoru Yamasaki's World Trade Center, which at the time of its ribbon cutting in 1973 had cost the Port Authority $900 million, a vast flow of capital from public to private coffers (Cudahy chapter 3). Harvey is especially persuasive in arguing that this consolidation of the private sector, and of the class power that subtends it, was a reaction to the upheavals of the 1960s, in which the actions of both unions and students were seen by the business classes as disruptive to the steady flow of capital. It is the period in which CUNY began to charge tuition for the first time (45).[2]

These are the material conditions that obsess Ashbery throughout the middle period of his career, which I date from *The Double Dream of Spring* to *A Wave* (1984). The books at the center of this period are *Three Poems*, from 1972, and 1975's *Self-Portrait in a Convex Mirror*, which won Ashbery three major literary awards in a single year.[3] This chapter will linger with *Three Poems* and center on *Self-Portrait;* but it might be helpful to begin with part of a poem from *The Double Dream of Spring*, because the poems of that book, the first he wrote after moving to New York City at the end of a decade of foreign travel, most explicitly lay out the terms of the theme that will preoccupy him. "Definition of Blue" begins with lines that sound ironic, but the irony is shed as the poem homes in on its subject, which is how material superabundance produces a portrait of the artist as its aftereffect:

> The rise of capitalism parallels the advance of romanticism
> And the individual is dominant until the close of the nineteenth
>   century.
> In our own time, mass practices have sought to submerge the
>   personality
> By ignoring it, which has caused it instead to branch out in all
>   directions
> . . .
> But today there is no point in looking to imaginative new methods
> Since all of them are in constant use. The most that can be said for them
>   further
> Is that erosion produces a kind of dust or exaggerated pumice

Which fills space and transforms it, becoming a medium
In which it is possible to recognize oneself.

(211)

The postromantic subject whose portrait is painted by the "pumice" of "mass practices" has no respite from that portraiture—indeed, he feels dragged into it. And he is not shy about identifying the social processes that "mass practices" entail. In a poem called "Decoy," which starts off as close to a declaration or a manifesto as anything Ashbery has ever produced, the poet writes:

We hold these truths to be self-evident:
That ostracism, both political and moral, has
Its place in the twentieth-century scheme of things;
That urban chaos is the problem we have been seeing into and seeing
  into,
For the factory, deadpanned by its very existence into a
Descending code of values, has moved right across the road from total
  financial upheaval
And caught regression head-on

(195)

In these lines Ashbery senses a collision between industry and finance ("the factory" and "total financial upheaval") in which both end up "regressing"—a movement that seems to be measured by "urban chaos," the letting of the city slide into disarray. This of course describes exactly the parameters of the struggle over American cities in the seventies: would they remain industrial, or become financial? Meanwhile, the "ostracism" he describes for those who would choose neither industry nor finance is elaborated in companion poems like "Soonest Mended," which begins by describing something like the struggles of a bohemian subculture on the margins of the city:

Barely tolerated, living on the margin
In our technological society, we were always having to be rescued
On the brink of destruction

(184)

Or here, in the opening lines of "Parergon," which describe (as per the title) the sheepish secondarity of literary labor:

> We are happy in our way of life.
> It doesn't make much sense to others. We sit about,
> Read, and are restless.
>
> (212)

Skipping around a bit, then, we can actually learn a little from the reticent Ashbery about his relation to this period in New York's history. And sometimes he is even more forthcoming: in a 2005 interview in the UK *Guardian,* he recalls winning the Pulitzer Prize, the National Book Critics Circle Award, and the National Book Award for *Self-Portrait,* and contextualizes his winning against the backdrop of the city's financial crises: "Those prizes were very welcome. I think I was probably going to get fired from Brooklyn College as New York was retrenching but instead I was given tenure." This modesty is paired with a bit of mischief when he recalls his participation in protests against the Vietnam War: "I went on the huge Central Park demonstration against the war when we marched to the UN, although me and my friends did stop off at a hotel bar to have a few margaritas on the way" (Wroe, "Parallel Lines").

I'm especially interested in this second comment, because it reflects something crucial to Ashbery's poetry of the 1970s, which is his belief in what he calls "wandering away." Again and again in the poems from this period, the poet describes scenes of spectacle, pageantry, and even apocalypse, which are made harmless by the poet's turning to face the other way, or drifting in a different direction. But the two comments are perhaps best taken together, because the poet who wanders away from the great events, from the looming catastrophes and conflicts, does not want us to see him as imperious; he wants us to recognize his smallness, his minority—he wants us to know that he is in danger, like any of us, of being downsized.

This posture of minority is reflected in Ashbery's career-long devotion to what he calls "The Other Tradition" of eccentric, uncanonizable poets as models for his own work, but it is not only a puckish resistance to classicality. It also encodes a wish not to be party to violence, which shades into a wish not to be responsible for it, which shades into a wish not to know about it. This uneasy dynamic is expressed through countless figures of looming disaster that the poet believes he can simply choose to "wander away" from.

Ashbery has remained invested enough in this minority poetics to have titled the 2000 collection of his Norton lectures at Harvard "Other Traditions"; those essays focus on "minor" poets like Laura Riding, John Wheelwright, and Thomas Lovell Beddoes. But Ashbery's interest in poetic minority is not only about the formation of a countercanon, or even the critique of canonicity; there is also a political component to it, a defense of apoliticality. In a poem from his 1977 volume *Houseboat Days* called "The Other Tradition," Ashbery depicts a scene of political gathering in which he distractedly participates, but from which, finally, he demurs. The poem begins:

> They all came, wore sentiments
> Emblazoned on T-shirts, proclaiming the lateness
> Of the hour, and indeed the sun slanted its rays
> Through branches of North Island pine as though
> Politely clearing its throat, and all ideas settled
> In a fuzz of dust under trees when it's drizzling

Though the T-shirts he sees are calls for action, Ashbery quickly translates "the lateness of the hour" into an atmospherics, a pathetic fallacy in which the sun, no activist, "politely [clears] its throat," and political ideas, like the "pumice" capital made of all recycled postures in the poem "Decoy," become a "fuzz of dust." It is simpler, the poet decides as he concludes the poem, to look the other way:

> You found this
> Charming, but turned your face fully toward night,
> Speaking into it like a megaphone, not hearing
> Or caring, although these still live and are generous
> And all ways contained, allowed to come and go
> Indefinitely in and out of the stockade
> They have so much trouble remembering, when our forgetting
> Rescues them at last, as a star absorbs the night.
>
> (491–492)

Only the word "megaphone" remains of the political scene, which has been translated into gentle natural inevitabilities, the "fuzz of dust" consolidated into a figure of the mingling of light and dark between a star and its surround. One must "forget" one's conditions, specifically that one is caught in a "stockade."

This resistance to politics in poetry is deep and very principled for Ashbery. In a letter to *The Nation* written after the death of Frank O'Hara,

Ashbery praised O'Hara for not having become a doctrinaire poet even though he had lived in ideologically supercharged times; for these remarks he was chastised by Louis Simpson, who felt Ashbery was praising political apathy and nonengagement. James Longenbach has uncovered Ashbery's response to this accusation, which also appeared in *The Nation*, and in which Ashbery says this:

> All poetry is against war and in favor of life, or else it isn't poetry, and it stops being poetry when it is forced into the mold of a particular program. Poetry is poetry. Protest is protest. I believe in both forms of action. (Longenbach, "Ashbery and the Individual Talent," 104)

So on the one hand we have an appealing insistence that poetry is a kind of antiviolence, and on the other we have a bracing reminder that poets, whatever their dreams of prophetic legislation, are minor, even minute, players on the contemporary political stage. In this argument, poetry is political simply by virtue of not being war; and poets are able to do what they do best when they are under no pressure to be "political."

But this argument is too easy, and Ashbery knows it: don't politics assert themselves in poetry sometimes, regardless of the poet's desires? At the end of "Decoy," he can't stop wondering what the agents of capital are really like; he can't keep himself from trying to understand the vast causal movements that produce "urban chaos" in more human terms:

> There is every reason to rejoice with those self-styled prophets of
> commercial disaster, those harbingers of gloom,
> Over the imminent lateness of the denouement that, advancing slowly,
> never arrives,
> At the same time keeping the door open to a tongue-and-cheek attitude
> on the part of the perpetrators,
> The men who sit down to their vast desks on Monday to being planning
> the week's notations, jotting memoranda that take
> Invisible form in the air, like flocks of sparrows
> Above the city pavements, turning and wheeling aimlessly
> But on the average by discernible motives.
>
> (195–196)

The attitude Ashbery is testing out here will become central to his poetry throughout the 1970s and into the early 1980s. Just as, at the beginning of "Decoy," the "factory" and "total financial upheaval" collide to make "regression," here, at the end of the poem, the men of finance meet a type of time that, though it looks like doom, actually spells reprieve: "the denouement that, advancing slowly, never arrives." Like the activist T-shirts announcing "the lateness of the hour" in "The Other Tradition," the bankers' memoranda announce a "commercial disaster" that never quite arrives—because, Ashbery wants to suggest, that's just how time *works*. Finance and activism alike, he is beginning to argue, are built around the expectation of punctual event (revolt, the realization of value), when in fact time works more fluidly than punctually, turning assertions into a "fuzz of dust," or dire fiscal predictions into the aimless "wheeling" of birds in the sky. This is why, despite his obvious outrage at the smug destructiveness of the "harbingers of gloom," he insists there is "reason to rejoice" at the work they do, because it turns out to be caught up in a type of time that will give the lie to all of their apocalypses.

Despite the minority poetics to which this idea of fluid time is attached in Ashbery, it has an arguably major pedigree. T. S. Eliot begins *Four Quartets* with exactly this Heraclitean theme, warning against the impulse to "redeem" time, to profit from it:

> Time present and time past
> Are both perhaps present in time future,
> And time future contained in time past.
> If all time is eternally present
> All time is unredeemable.
>
> (*Collected Poems*, 175)

In Eliot, of course, this argument for time-as-flux is related to religious austerity: recognizing time's fluidity is an aid toward ending "Attachment to self" (205). This austerity is alien to Ashbery; but closer to home, in the poems of Wallace Stevens, there is a career-long insistence on flux in which apocalypse is seen as bluster, or as self-involvement—as with the protagonist of "The Doctor of Geneva," who converts the alien sublimity of the Pacific into a purely rhetorical apotheosis. The Doctor feels no awe in the face of the sea, Stevens writes, but he is still most willing to make use of its tumults,

> Which yet found means to set his simmering mind
> Spinning and hissing with oracular
> Notations of the wild, the ruinous waste,

> Until the steeples of his city clanked and sprang
> In an unburgherly apocalypse.
> The doctor used his handkerchief and sighed.
>
> (*Collected Poems,* 24)

This light satire of the apocalyptic cast of mind, which Longenbach has glossed extensively in Stevens, finds more emphatic form in "Extracts from Addresses to the Academy of Fine Ideas," where the willingness not to project too much onto the world, or to desire too much from its stimuli, allows one to "[resist] each past apocalypse" (257). And in "An Ordinary Evening in New Haven," the movement of the days and the seasons are made to feel part of "a permanence composed of impermanence" (472) that makes moot the self-involvement of human apportionings of matter:

> Why, then, inquire
> Who has divided the world, what entrepreneur?
> No man.
>
> (468)

Like the "self-styled prophets of commercial disaster" in Ashbery's "Decoy," Stevens's burghers and entrepreneurs take themselves too seriously and miss the essential folly of trying to divvy up space, or portion out time, in a Heraclitean world. For Stevens, strolling New Haven in 1949, this was clearly a pleasing thought. For Ashbery, it has more the air of desperate reassurance—not least because the power to apportion, to divide, and to accumulate had helped produce an urban crisis by the 1970s.

Does accumulation breed disaster? This is the question Ashbery worries about in *Three Poems,* which is the volume where he first describes the possibility of an "other tradition":

> There wasn't too much of any one thing. The feelings never wandered off into a private song or tried to present the procession of straightforward facts as something like a pageant: the gorgeous was still unknown. There was, however, a residue, a kind of fiction that developed parallel to the classic truths of daily life (as it was in that heroic but commonplace age) as they unfolded with the foreseeable majesty of a holocaust, an unfrightening one, and went unrecognized, drawing force and grandeur

> from this like the illegitimate offspring of a king. It is this "other tradition" which we propose to explore. (281–282)

Like the "pumice" in "Decoy," or the "fuzz of dust" in "The Other Tradition," the "residue" that emerges in this passage alongside "the classic truths of daily life" is both a material by-product of that life and also the medium for another type of time, a counterapocalypse or a "holocaust" that's "unfrightening." It's the minority time of the "other tradition," that "sits about" instead of rushing, that skips the parade, as it were, avoiding "pageantry" in favor of an aimlessness that's "rescued" by "forgetting" the dread of the emerging spectacle. There is never "too much of any one thing" because *nothing accumulates.* Or, as Howard put it, the minor poems of this tradition seem only to move "around the column their own accumulation raises."

I think this is less a fact of the poems, though, than their wish, their nervous dream. From the very beginning of *Three Poems* it is clear that Ashbery wants very much for the political problems he's skirting to be understood as an abstract problem of accumulation per se, or as a problem of writerly composition:

> I thought that if I could put it all down, that would be one way. And next the thought came to me that to leave all out would be another, and truer, way. (247)

A bit later the poet shades in two related questions, of aggregation and of significance:

> I could still put everything in and have it come out even, that is have it come out so that you and I are equal at the end of our lives, which would have been lived fully and without strain. (253)

By the end of the book, however, this equanimity has been lost. Ashbery writes:

> Any reckoning of the sum total of the things we are is of course doomed to failure from the start, that is if it intends to present a true, wholly objective picture from which both artifice and artfulness are banished: no art can exist without at least traces of these . . . Perhaps no art . . . can supply what we were demanding of it: not only the figured representation of our days but the justification of them . . . so close to the reality being lived that it vanishes suddenly in a thunderclap, with a loud cry. (322)

This problem of sums and judgments is still being teased out in general terms, as a problem of art's relation to personhood, both single and collective. But it takes on a nervous bivalence. Midway through the book, for instance, the poet writes of an anonymous "he,"

> Thus summed up, he felt sickened at the wholeness (276).

Only to write, a page and a half later,

> He thought he had never seen anything quite so beautiful as that crystallization into a mountain of statistics . . . out of that river of humanity . . . a tonal quality detached itself that partook of the motley intense hues of the whole gathering but yet remained itself, firm and all-inclusive. (277–278)

The crowd, the "river of humanity," produces "tone" after the fashion of the other "residues" that are the giveaway markers for Ashbery's minority: something secondary, something alongside "statistics" but not captured by them. This is reassuring to the poet; but crowds being crowds, the feeling they produce is unmanageable, and may easily convert into something else, something that may be too much to bear:

> Who are all these people? What does it mean that there are so many? . . .
> It may become necessary to shut them all out. (275)

He tries to preserve a residual sense of safety with regard to his theme of not getting bogged down in the details, posing it as the forgivable failure to make add up what can't be:

> What about the morning resolutions to convert all the confused details in the air about you into a column of intelligible figures? To draw up a balance sheet? (289)

But this easy problem repeatedly modulates into a hard one, the one that prompts the poet's desire to shut people out, to wander away. The hard problem is that the overwhelming, terrifying spectacles draw on the same energy, and have the same structure, as the very sources of aesthetic experience, the wellsprings of the poetry. It takes placing two passages alongside each other really to see this. Consider these:

> But the light continues to grow, the eternal disarray of sunrise, and one can now distinguish certain shapes such as haystacks and a clocktower.

> So it was true, everything was holding its breath because a surprise was on the way. It has already installed itself and begun to give orders: workmen are struggling to raise the main pole that supports the tent while over there others are watering the elephants, dressing down the horses; one is pretending to box with a tame bear. Everything is being lifted or locked into place all over the vast plain, without fuss or worry it slowly nears completion thanks to exceptional teamwork on the part of the crew of roustabouts and saltimbanques whose job this was anyway, and whose ardor need never have excited any jealousy on your part: they are being paid, after all. And one moves closer, drawn first by the aura of the spectacle, to come to examine the merit of its individual parts so as to enjoy even more connecting them up to the whole. (274)

And:

> But it dawned on him all of a sudden that there was another way, that this horrible vision of the completed Tower of Babel, flushed in the sunset as the last ceramic brick was triumphantly fitted into place, perfect in its vulgarity, an eternal reminder of the advantages of industry and cleverness—that the terror could be shut out—and really shut out—simply by turning one's back on it. (279)

These two excerpts make good bookends, one of them set at sunrise and one at sunset. Both describe the spectacular character of a great labor, some work of "locking" or "fitting" things "into place," though in the first passage a circus has come to town, and the assembly is the assembly of its tents, while the second passage describes the completion of a monument, a ziggurat. The first passage describes a scene from village life, while the second is archetypically urban. And the first passage, in which the "aura of the spectacle" is alluring rather than terrifying, depicts a collective labor in which workers are actually visible, whereas they aren't to be found in the second passage, except in the phrase "the last ceramic brick was triumphantly fitted into place"—where "triumph" is more about the realization of the dream of the tyrant Nimrod than about the satisfaction of whichever slave laid the last brick.

Morning versus evening; a temporary structure versus a monument; day-labor versus slavery: lined up with the figures we've seen so far for poetic minority, these contrasts begin to establish a textual network in which Ashbery can make a bid for the harmless and noncumulative labor of writing without having to stage a full-scale argument on writing's behalf. He is building a textual "matter," you could say, that works more by cross-reference than by argument, more by the recurrence of topoi than by syllogism. The beautifully exploratory prose of *Three Poems* gave Ashbery the compositional space in which to bring these topoi alongside each other without bringing them too close, without having to seem to insist on his minority, his demurrals. In *Self-Portrait in a Convex Mirror,* however, he comes as close as he ever will to making a case for them.

Across the course of thirty-five freestanding poems, *Self-Portrait* stages a drama that pits punctual events against flux, looming catastrophe against the subtlety of mood, apocalypse against dailiness. The range of emotion attached to these contrasts varies considerably. In the first poem in the book, Ashbery describes

> That time when one can no longer wander away
> And even the least attentive fall silent
> To watch the thing that is prepared to happen
>
> ("As One Put Drunk into the Packet-Boat," 427)

There is a sense of excitement in the dignity of the event, which takes on the shadings of a performance:

> The great, formal affair was beginning . . .
> That takes in the whole world, now, but lightly,
> Still lightly, but with wide authority and tact.

The spectacle that "takes in the whole world" compels attendance, here, for something like its beauty, for the "lightness" of its "authority and tact"—no one would want to "wander away" from it. Elsewhere, though, the great event is more threatening:

> your house is built in tomorrow
> but surely not before the examination
> of what is right and will befall
> not before the census
> and the writing down of names
> remember you are free to wander away
> as from other times other scenes that were taking place . . .

it is finally as though that thing of monstrous interest
were happening in the sky
but the sun is setting and prevents you from seeing it
("As You Came from the Holy Land," 430)

In this scene of biblical judgment, "wander[ing] away" is less a failing of the inattentive than a strategy of the frightened. Drifting elsewhere, combined with the fortuitousness of the sunset obscuring the "monstrous event," allows the speaker not to confront whatever it is that looms as "the seasons change and tremble" (430).

Sometimes this dynamic of looming event is phrased in terms of the cruelty of narrative. The poems meditate endlessly on storytelling, especially on fairy tales and other forms "steeped in the nostalgia of a collective past" ("Self-Portrait," 482). In "Scheherazade," Ashbery notes with alarm the "extremity" of received narrative forms, whose "possibilities are limited":

It is seen
At the end that the kind and good are rewarded,
That the unjust one is doomed to burn forever
Around his error, sadder and wiser anyway.
(433)

Against this scene of judgment, in which the arcs of stories mete out justice with no remainder, Ashbery poses the existence of what lies outside the story's arc—both "the minor characters," whom he says "must be kept in mind," and the story's audience. "What would they be," he asks about stories,

Without an audience to restrict the innumerable
Passes and swipes, restored to good humor as it issues
Into the impervious evening air?
(433–434)

What's outside the story—especially, you might say, the social relationships around its consumption—is depended upon to prevent narrative from becoming merciless. Having shown us the eternal damnation of the "unjust one" in the middle of the poem, Ashbery alters the scene at its close:

So in some way
Although the arithmetic is incorrect

The balance is restored because it
Balances, knowing it prevails,
And the man who made the same mistake twice is exonerated.

(434)

There is a recurring anxiety in the poems about whether, indeed, "the arithmetic is incorrect," or, more precisely, whether a patently incorrect arithmetic can be allowed to pass. In a short poem, "Foreboding," Ashbery renders this as a schoolyard scene, in which we find

A big ugly one
With braces kicking the shit out of a smaller one
Who reaches for a platinum axe stamped excalibur

The poet, witnessing the scene, can't undo the violence; he writes:

I feel as though
Somebody had just brought me an equation.
I say, "I can't answer this—I know
That it's true, please believe me,
I can see the proof, lofty, invisible
In the sky far above the striped awnings. I just see
That I want it to go on, without
Anybody's getting hurt

(452)

The spectacle of bullying, which can be halted only by solving an equation whose "proof" remains invisible in the "sky," is not only part of a network of figures of sums; it is also contributes to an array of sky and aerial figures in *Self-Portrait,* in which the sky as scene of judgment is nervously contrasted with the weather that alters it, or with the humble, minor action on the ground, or with the ability to turn away. In "Absolute Clearance," the speaker imagines he must "suffer again the light to be displaced," a light that takes the form of a merciless eagle falling "so surely on its prey/That one can avoid its nails/No less than its eyes" (435). No sooner has he imagined this aerial judgment, though, than he proposes an alternative to himself:

How it would be clearer
Just to loaf, imagining little
(The fur of a cat in the sun):
Let the column of figures

Shift, add and subtract itself
(Sticks, numbers, letters)
And so on to median depth

(435)

Scenes like this, in which merciless calculation is seen as coming from above, but also as somehow avoidable, create a strange sense of what we might call optional apocalypse, in which a judgment, or crisis, is simply walked away from, or converted from looming catastrophe to consumable spectacle by the choice of spectatorship: it is eventually assumed that the incorrect sums will add up anyway, that the figures will balance, that no one will get hurt.

Sometimes this choice of nonapocalypse is explicitly contrasted with the exigencies of social organization, as in the poem "No Way of Knowing":

Anyway evening
Kind of changes things. Not the color,
The quality of a handshake, the edge on someone's breath
So much as a general anxiety to get everything all added up,
Flowers arranged and out of sight. The vehicular madness
Goes on, crashing, thrashing away, but
For many this is near enough to the end: one may
Draw up a chair close to the balcony railing.
The sunset is just starting to light up.

(465)

Once again sunset comes to the rescue, allowing those who have chosen to opt out of "the vehicular madness" that is careering toward some frightening "end" to consume instead a quieter event in the sky.

These arbitrary rescues are haunted by the question of who gets to opt out of violence: more often than not, those who have no choice but to suffer are imagined as far away, or indiscernible. Sometimes the poet is explicit: reeling out a latter-day fairytale about "the water of life" in the poem called "Oleum Misericordae," he marvels how an ironic-heroic "you" manages, through a series of "chance encounter[s]," to get the magical liquid "safely home," "[save] the old man's life" and "[inherit] the kingdom." But then he writes:

But this was just a moment
Under the most cheerful sun.

In poorer lands
No one touches the water of life.

(473)

In other poems "the poorer lands" do not bear specifying, or not quite. In "Grand Galop," the poet writes:

And so from a day replete with rumors
Of things being done on the other side of the mountains
A nucleus remains, a still-perfect possibility
That can be kept indefinitely. And yet
The groans of labor pains are deafening

(440)

Here the poet implicitly poses the besieged clarity of that "nucleus of possibility" against the "rumors" and the "groans" that tell tales about the ominously unspecified "things being done on the other side of the mountains," and his concern is to preserve that nucleus of "possibility," even if preserving it amounts to a state of enforced isolation. In the poem called "Voyage in the Blue," he refers to "our closed-in state," and hopes that one day the vague concern he shares with others will come to seem "remote, like a catastrophe / In some unheard-of country" (446). Later in that same poem, he worries over exactly his ability to be alive and perceiving in the world, where alertness gives view to "The painful freshness of each thing being exactly itself." Preferable to this alertness seems to be the attitude toward death of the elderly, who "want no part of us, / Only to be dying, and over with it." Ashbery gives the asocial elderly center stage for the rest of the poem, where they are depicted as preferring to think about the long durée of which they are coming to form a part, rather than the individual events that disturb their peace:

It is civilization that counts, after all, they seem
To be saying, and we are as much a part of it as anybody else
Only we think less about it even not at all, until some
Fool comes shouting into the forest at nightfall
News of some thing we know and care little of

(447)

We do not learn the content of this "news," just as it is kept from us in other poems. But Ashbery is endlessly deft in allegorizing the *motion* of the news—the movement of its situation, where and how it takes place. In the lines that follow the ones I've just cited—lines that close the poem—the fool's announcement is met with pleasure in "the distant castle,"

> releasing rooks straight up into the faultless air
> And meanwhile weighs its shadow ever heavier on the mirroring
> Surface of the river, surrounding the little boat with three figures in it.

Though brief, this closing situation of the "news" is dense with reference—from the "faultless air," another figure among many for the sky's ambiguous status as scene of both judgment and reprieve, to the "mirroring surface of the river," here as elsewhere in the book as figure for a Heraclitean flux that outmaneuvers punctual events but also isolates those in the water, as it does here, "surrounding the little boat with three figures in it." This fairytale diorama encapsulates a key dynamic at work in *Self-Portrait,* in which the phenomenology of dailiness, its flux, its shifts in mood, are counterposed to the frightening public world of punctual event, of "news." This counterposition happens many ways, with a wide array of valences, and is often called into play with a very self-conscious, I think even a guilty, arbitrariness. The confrontation of the punctual with the fluid, freighted with public-private connotations, is arguably the book's central problem; I would like to spend some time now tracking how, in repeatedly posing it, Ashbery tries to understand it.

The first thing worth noticing about Ashbery's approach in *Self-Portrait* to the strain in time between punctuality and flux, public and private, apocalypse and "wandering away," is that he almost always puzzles over the question with reference to the times of day. Indeed, just to review the passages I've highlighted so far is to be struck by the consistency with which this famously fluid poetics returns to the passage from morning to night. There is the "thing of monstrous interest" in the sky, in "As You Came from the Holy Land," which sunset prevents the poet from confronting; in "Scheherazade" there is "the impervious evening air" that provides space for potentially violent narrative to be "restored to good humor"; in "No Way of Knowing," we hear that "evening kind of changes things" for how it triggers a "general anxiety to get everything all added up"; in "Grand Galop," the remains of the day carry a residue of disturbing news, "from a day replete with rumor / Of things being done on the other side of the mountains";

and, of course, in "Voyage in the Blue" the peace of the fairytale village of poetry is disturbed by the "Fool" who "comes shouting into the forest at nightfall." Anxiety, reprieve, the avoidance of bad news, its unavoidability—all these gather at the ends of days. This is perhaps because what comes after evening—that is, nighttime—is conceived in *Self-Portrait* as a time of refreshment. In "Voyage in the Blue" Ashbery writes, "Into our darkness life seeps, / Keeping its part of the bargain" (445). And, of course, there are the resounding last lines of "As One Put Drunk into the Packet-Boat":

> The summer demands and takes away too much,
> But night, the reserved, the reticent, gives more than it takes.
>
> (428)

In both these passages of nighttime, the "general anxiety" of evening is supplanted by a fortuitous economic arrangement, a "bargain," in which the poetic subject may given life at no cost, or possibly at a profit. Again, though, the poet feels guilty about celebrating such advantageous arrangements; later in the book, he reworks the grateful paean of "As One Put Drunk" with the same cadence, but self-damningly:

> Morning is for sissies like you
> But the real trials, the ones that separate the men from the boys, come later.
>
> (440)

The movement of the day, then, from morning to evening to nightfall, carries the weight of a dilemma about "the real trials," sometimes figured as a distant catastrophe, sheepishly avoided, sometimes figured as the problem of needing to make a sum add up correctly when it patently won't. Across the course of the book this return to the language of day, evening, and night is tied to questions about what one can accomplish, in a day, or to questions of what a day's passage can be said to measure: "So much we could have done, / So much we did do," the poet writes in "Poem in Three Parts," the two lines resting atop each other as if in ratio. Or, in another section of the same poem,

> There are so many different jobs:
> It's sufficient to choose one, or a fraction of one.
> Days will be blue elsewhere with their own purpose.
>
> (443)

Another "bargain" is struck here, between the fractional activity of the poet and the "purpose" of the "days," which keep their own counsel. The independent relation between the two things—the poet's "job" and the telos of the day—is rendered here as a statement, but for Ashbery the relationship is quite fraught: there is no guarantee that the "days" will put no pressure on work, or demand no "purpose" from the sheepishly self-isolating poet.

"Grand Galop" is the poem that worries this question most thoroughly, expanding it into a meditation on how the labor of perception is parceled out in social systems that feel too complex actually to be perceived. Here is the poet, contemplating the "general anxiety" of evening once more:

> As long as one has some sense that each thing knows its place
> All is well, but with the arrival and departure
> Of each new one overlapping so intensely in the semi-darkness
> It's a bit mad. Too bad, I mean, that getting to know each just for a
> fleeting second
> Must be replaced by imperfect knowledge of the featureless whole,
> Like some pocket history of the world, so general
> As to constitute a sob or wail unrelated
> To any attempt at definition.
>
> (437–438)

At the beginning of "As One Put Drunk into the Packet-Boat," the poet "tried each thing," finding "only some were immortal and free." Here "each thing knows its place" only intermittently because it is part of a "mad" play of "arrival and departure"—a "vehicular madness," you could say—that obliges the observer to generalize each "each" into a "featureless whole," whose generality does no justice to the particulars it rounds. Indeed, the only sound the "featureless whole" can make is an unpoetic "sob or wail" that rings all too uncomfortably with the "groan" of the dark deeds being done "on the other side of the mountains."

This upset meditation on the failed generality of "some pocket history of the world" continues in lines that return to the question of the "minor"—this time, not only the "minor characters" who prevent narrative from becoming brutal, but also the histories they form:

> And the minor eras
> Take on an importance out of all proportion to the story
> For it can no longer unwind, but must be kept on hand

Indefinitely, like a first-aid kit no one ever uses
Or a word in the dictionary that no one will ever look up.
The custard is setting; meanwhile
I not only have my own history to worry about
But am forced to fret over insufficient details related to huge
Unfinished concepts that can never bring themselves to the point
Of being, with or without my help, if any were forthcoming.
(438)

That "the minor eras" of this passage double as "the minor characters" with whom Ashbery feels himself allied is made clear when he introduces the problem of his "own history," to which is painfully superadded the problem of his contribution to an unfinished, perhaps unfinishable, whole. He finds himself uncomfortably part of a reserve army of conceptual labor, a one-person "minor era" kept in the background like a first-aid kit or rare word, with responsibility for the historical whole but no power to shape it. Like the protestations of helplessness we saw earlier, this complaint is staged as a matter of time and its pressures, which string the poet between the "fleeting second" of his capacities and the "indefinite" longeur of his being held in reserve by a system from which he cannot, it turns out, "wander away."

Why, then, does he? If the inevitable movement of morning into day's demands, and evening's worries, prevents the poet from arriving without anxiety at "reserved," refreshing night, if the unsolvable equation, the terminally bad math, cannot be expunged from the arc of the poetic "day," how does Ashbery find license to produce so many figures of demurral?

The answer seems to lie in the kind of time produced by living in shadow of the spectacles that dot the book. The demands of "each thing" rushing by, congealing into threat and dissolving into harmlessness—these demands are so perpetual that they have the contradictory effect of freeing the poet to do nothing at all, of leaving him with time on his hands. Enmeshed in an unfinishable collective labor, endlessly solicited by the comings and goings of each thing but kept perpetually in reserve, the poet feels he has access to the option of "wandering away" from violence, from catastrophe, from the news, precisely because he experiences himself as having been made so powerless by the stream of the spectacle.

That, at least, is the claim. In "Tenth Symphony," whose title signifies unfinishable work (the tenth is the symphony even the greatest nineteenth-century composers were said to be unable to complete), Ashbery begins by saying what he hasn't yet said: "I have not told you / About the riffraff at the boat show." This spectacle, "All red and white and blue and red," like a self-restarting American flag, or an angry one, leads the poet to think about sex and excess:

> You've never told me about a lot of things:
> Why you love me, why we love you, and just exactly
> What sex is. When people speak of it
> As happens increasingly, are they always
> Referring to the kind where sexual organs are brought in—
> Diffident, vague, difficult to imagine as they are to a blind person?
> I find that thinking these things divides us,
> Brings us together. As on last Thanksgiving
> Nobody could finish what was on his plate,
> And gave thanks.
>
> (458)

The too-muchness of the ruddy boat show, its undescribability, is made to seem like an erotic language on the "increase," whose frequency and rising specificity breeds its opposite, a shyness about details, which links people in an inability to finish the description of whatever sex might actually be: it "divides us, / Brings us together." What's left is a too-large meal, an uncomfortable surplus and an unfinishable labor that, if it "divides" those who consume it, at least "beings them together" in their alienation.

The figures shift quickly: boat show, sex, food. But, Ashbery says,

> There is some connexion
> . . .
> Among this. It connects up,
> Not *to* anything, but kind of like
> Closing ranks so as to leave them open.
> You can "stop and shop." Self service
> And the honor system prevail, resulting in
> Tremendous amounts of spare time,
> A boon to some, to others more of a problem
> That only points a way around it.
>
> (459)

Now the problem of free time, surplus, and relief in shared alienation is understood as a system-situation, in which one lives with a connectivity that doesn't lead anywhere but connects for its own sake, creating an enclosure inside which everything is free, or nearly free. The stasis this breeds is itself activity: "You can 'stop and shop.'" Not everyone can turn the experience of enclosed liberation to a worthy end, but the poet knows what to do:

Sitting in the living room this afternoon I saw
How to use it. My vision remained etched in the
Buff wall a long time, an elective
Cheshire cat. Unable to cancel,
The message is received penultimately.

Turning his surplus into use value, the poet immediately disappears. Not only does he become a "Cheshire cat," but the "I" in his statement "I saw / How to use it," unusually emphatic for the Ashbery of *Self-Portrait,* disappears into "my vision," and then into the uncertain agency of "unable to cancel," which may refer either to the poet or to "the message" he receives after staring into the buff-colored wall. His "elective" passivity turns that wall into a kind of ballot, whose enclosing emptiness allows the poet to experience his passivity as action, as choice, perhaps because it takes effort to withstand the stream of that which one is "unable to cancel": in the poem immediately preceding "Tenth Symphony," called "The One Thing That Can Save America," Ashbery describes the place-names of the American landscape "beating themselves into eyes which have had enough / Thank you, no more thank you" (457).

In any case "Tenth Symphony" concludes with an ironic negation of the poet's claim to have figured out how to use his spare time:

So over these past years—
A little puttering around,
Some relaxing, a lot of plans and ideas.
Hope to have more time to tell you about
The latter in the foreseeable future.

(459)

This dithering-away, the hope for "more time" in a scene already tagged as all too full of time, marks a final self-canceling, a "wandering away," you could say, from the critical impulse that began the poem. Betting on futures in a society glutted with them, the poem's ironic conclusion suggests, is a losing game.

Perhaps this is why Ashbery reserves more pathos for his reflections, not on the future, but on the past. In "Absolute Clearance," whose title suggests the sweeping away of what's just been made obsolete, he notices ruefully

> The times when a slow horse along
> A canal bank seems irrelevant and the truth:
> The best in its sample
> Of time in relation to other time.
>
> (434)

The figure of the horse returns in "Ode to Bill," a landscape poem that worries over whether writing is really work:

> One horse stands out irregularly against
> The land over there. And am I receiving
> This vision? Is it mine, or do I already owe it
> For other visions, unnoticed and unrecorded
> On the great, relaxed curve of time,
> All the forgotten springs, dropped pebbles,
> Songs once heard then passed out of light
> Into everyday oblivion? He moves slowly away,
> Looks up and pumps the sky, a lingering
> Question. Him too we can sacrifice
> To the end progress, for we must, we must be moving on.
>
> (462)

Here the figure of the horse congeals a sense of guilty indebtedness to earlier forms of labor (buried in the figure from "Absolute Clearance," slowly pulling goods along the Erie Canal) that is the flip side of having "tremendous amounts of spare time." The mute "question" formed by the movement of the horse's body recalls once more the animals in Auden's Freud elegy, silently begging to be allowed to participate in Enlightenment, the animals whom Auden fervently hoped we would not forsake "to the end progress."

Throughout the poems that make up the first three-fourths of *Self-Portrait in a Convex Mirror,* Ashbery repeatedly and guiltily asserts that he lives in a world of perpetually looming disasters that he is able to avoid by dint of walking away, or turning the other direction, or waiting for the next thing to happen, or repositioning himself as the spectator of disaster rather than as its victim. Sometimes his assertion of safety or harmlessness is self-damning, as in "Tenth Symphony" or in parts of "Grand Galop"; sometimes it is peevish, as in the proxy irritation the poet's fairy-tale elders feel for the "fool" who disturbs the peace of the poetic forest in "Voyage in the Blue"; and sometimes it is simply lyric, as with the sunset in "No Way of Knowing," or the gorgeous final lines about the generosity of nighttime in "As One Put Drunk into the Packet-Boat." In all of these cases Ashbery relies on the notion that time is fluid in order to dodge the implications of punctual, public event, especially event that takes spectacular form. The problem with this tactic for the book is that, as Ashbery continues to deploy it at the level of poetic argument, it begins to feel wishful, or excessive, like a fairy tale in which the princess is miraculously rescued by the dashing prince not once, not twice, but seven, eight, nine times. In the final poem in the book, however—the long title poem—Ashbery at last forgoes the arbitrary comforts of the optional apocalypse. In that famous poem, as we will see, the fluidity of time is less a refuge from the terrors of the spectacle than its enabling condition.

"Self-Portrait in a Convex Mirror" is inspired by Parmigianino's painting of the same name, roughly dated 1524. In six long strophes, Ashbery plumbs the implications of the painter's painstaking representation of the distortions of figure produced by a curved mirror. He finds in the portrait an extremely generative source for thinking about the relationship between fluidity and imprisonment—for thinking about how forms that are free to distort themselves, to compose a whole that is "stable within instability," nonetheless reduce to a "uniform substance, a magma of interiors" (476, 477). For Ashbery, the painting's inclusion of distortion in a realist vocabulary implies something frightening for its viewers:

> that the soul is not a soul,
> Has no secret, is small, and it fits
> Its hollow perfectly: its room, our moment of attention.
>
> (475)

Inasmuch as imagining oneself as the subject of the portrait comprises even a "moment of attention," to envision oneself englobed but not literally caged is to feel oneself structurally imprisoned: not as soul-substance different in kind from, and artificially restrained by, mundane material, but simply as part of that material, the whirr of whose distortions gives one a sense of vertigo that is queasily cousin to freedom.

The shock of the painting for Ashbery, then, is the shock of recognizing a kind of imprisonment that seems, until we are brought face to face with its structural distortions, like nature itself, like being free. This recognition leads to another line of meditation in the poem, about the historical distance between the painting and its viewer, between the 1520s and the 1970s, and about what kind of object the painting has now become. Indeed, I think in his way Ashbery is trying to historicize the painting, if by "historicize" we can mean the attempt to understand what unsolved problems the painting bequeaths its latter-day viewers. Imagining himself within the scene of the painting—that is, in Parmigianino's studio—Ashbery sees he cannot break out of the curvature of its space from within:

> One would like to stick one's hand
> Out of the globe, but its dimension,
> what carries it, will not allow it.
>
> (475)

Here Ashbery suggests, with extraordinary precision, that this globe of "magma" is not imprisoning because it is walled in, but because the "dimension" of the globe, something like its quality as globe and also its actual curvature, prevents escape. This unstable use of the word "dimension"—as measure, as aspect—is modified by "what carries it," which is to say that Ashbery renders the studio's, the painting's, englobed character as the result of an ongoing action, invisible as such, but effective nonetheless. Ashbery feels the source of his entrapment, not in the globe shape per se, but in a continuous and invisible action that makes the globe englobed.

This entrapment leads Ashbery, staring at a postcard of the painting at his desk, to try to regain his balance by distancing himself from the painting's curved world; but this effort produces a different kind of unease, the vertigo of historical time accelerating between them:

> I feel the carousel starting slowly
> And going faster: desk, papers, books,
> Photographs of friends, the window and the trees
> Merging in one neutral band that surrounds
> Me on all sides
> . . .
>   and as time speeds up so that it is soon
> Much later, I can know only the straight way out,
> The distance between us.
>
> (477)

Together these two passages establish a key problem of the poem, which is that in order not to feel made dizzy by the painting, trapped by its curvature, one must wriggle free by way of an even worse vertigo, a taking stock of historical distance that feels, confronting it, like the very opposite of history, like "one neutral band." This is to say that, though the earlier poems in *Self-Portrait* were virtuosic in their talent for finding ways to counterpose two types of time, the punctual and the fluid, in the title poem of the volume Ashbery begins by posing a much sterner problem to himself—not, how might flux outmaneuver punctual time, but, what if the attempt to dodge the spectacle by way of fluidity is the first step toward succumbing to the spectacle? What if fluidity is in fact both a source of life and a source of imprisonment? What if trying to locate oneself historically is nauseating?

Ashbery tries to answer these questions by returning to a figure from the earlier part of *Self-Portrait,* the figure of the magical sum. In the earlier poems, that self-correcting addition appeared as a kind of arbitrary reassurance, either in the form of deus ex machina ("I can see the proof, lofty, invisible / In the sky," in "Foreboding") or tautology ("Although the arithmetic is incorrect / The balance is restored because it / Balances," in "Scheherazade"). Here, though, the production of the magical sum is exactly the activity that captures and impoverishes all those who contemplate the portrait's globe:

more keeps getting included
Without adding to the sum, and just as one
Gets accustomed to a noise that
Kept one awake but now no longer does,
So the room contains this flow like an hourglass
Without varying in climate or quality
. . .
What should be the vacuum of a dream
Becomes continually replete as the source of dreams
Is being tapped so that this one dream
May wax, flourish like a cabbage rose,
Defying sumptuary laws, leaving us
To awake and try to begin living in what
Has now become a slum.

(478)

This grim movement from "sum" to "slum" drags everything with it, including the word and the idea of the "climate," earlier a wobbly figure of collective safety ("but for the time being we are free / And meanwhile the songs / Protect us, in a way, and the special climate," in "Robin Hood's Barn," 470). More immediately frightening, though, is the vampiric language for the operation of the unchanging but ever-absorptive "sum," which taps into the sleeping subject and with the energy it finds there arrogates all radiance to itself, bursting past old forms of apportionment for glory and creating the "slum" in its wake.

This process is frightening because it is gentle, and because the sleepy subject, waking, seems to consent to the new conditions the self-altering sum has left behind—the slum, or worse, a replica of the city, of life in the city. The poet eyes the painting:

> The forms retain a strong measure of ideal beauty
> As they forage in secret on our idea of distortion.
> Why be unhappy with this arrangement, since
> Dreams prolong us as they are absorbed?
> Something like living occurs, a movement
> Out of the dream into its codification.
>
> (478–479)

Cumulatively, the curvature of the painting's forms produces distortions—a huge hand, a receding torso—that aren't accurate to the body, but in any single interval of the eye's movement over the painting, those distortions seem normal, inevitable. To puzzle over this Zeno-like problem of the difference between a normal-seeming interval and a cumulative distortion is to become aware of their "foraging" on us, "tapping into" not only our "idea of distortion" but our vitality. Whereas in "Voyage in the Blue," Ashbery had written, "Into our darkness life seeps, / Keeping its part of the bargain," here that "bargain" has been replaced with an incremental extraction of life that replaces life with its replica: "something like living occurs."

The poet's acceptance of this simulation of life is a kind of climactic gesture, and it creates a formal problem for "Self-Portrait": how to conclude a poem that has thoroughly probed, and accepted, the conditions of its pseudolife? What is the poetic arc of resignation? Clearly elegy is an option, and poem does close with these lines, in which

each part of the whole falls off
And cannot know it knew, except
Here and there, in cold pockets
Of remembrance, whispers out of time.

(487)

But in order for this conclusion to obtain whatever pathos it is going to, Ashbery needs to bring the two activities the poem describes together: he needs to establish a relationship between the painterly work of Parmigianino and the slum-producing work in which "more keeps getting included / Without adding to the sum." Until now Ashbery has blurred the question of the social objectivity in Parmigianino's painting: he has suggested more than once that to observe the painting is to experience a truth, not only about its technical achievement, but about the sense of the world that the technique bequeaths us. He has spoken in the first-person plural about that bequeathal, about "our idea of distortion," and about how the painting leaves "us" to "begin living in what / Has now become a slum." And he has repeatedly suggested that the painting's technical achievement in making distortion seem like reality is akin to a collective experience of entrapment that he urgently needs to feel is benign. But he has shied away from making Parigianino's painting a mere example of a social process, undoubtedly because he is fascinated by the specificities of the painting, regardless of their uneasy resonance with life in the 1970s.

Now, though, under the pressure to give closure to his resignation, he imagines more specifically the work of englobement that the painting makes him recognize. How is the englobing activity of the painting like or unlike the "neutral band" that signifies contemporary enclosure?

Ashbery works out answers to these questions by way of a gradual leave-taking of the painting, and of Parmigianino, the poem's intermittent addressee. The poet wonders, first of all, whether there is anything specific to aesthetic experience, whether looking at the painting really means anything:

Yet the "poetic," straw-colored space
Of the long corridor that leads back to the painting,
Its darkening opposite—is this
Some figment of "art," not to be imagined
As real, let alone special?

(483)

Like the "buff-colored wall" from "Tenth Symphony," or the white noise "that / Kept one awake but now no longer does," the "straw-colored space" is a medium for an uncertain aesthetic autonomy—indeed, all three neutral tones describe the displacement of the aesthetic by something that smoothly terminates its specificity. The operation is so complete that it calls into question, not only the autonomy, but the reality, of aesthetic experience:

> Is there any point in acknowledging
> The existence of all that? Does it
> Exist? Certainly the leisure to
> Indulge stately pastimes doesn't,
> Any more. Today has no margins, the event arrives
> Flush with its edges, is of the same substance,
> Indistinguishable. "Play" is something else;
> It exists, in a society specifically
> Organized as a demonstration of itself.
>
> (484)

Without "margins" for reflection, leisure is codified into "play," a pseudoleisure in which event endlessly displaces event in the name of proving that the system—whatever it is—exists and functions; proving, as Ashbery himself puts it, "There is no other way." Or, more elaborately,

> There is no other way, and those assholes
> Who would confuse everything with their mirror games
> Which seem to multiply stakes and possibilities, or
> At least confuse issues by means of an investing
> Aura that would corrode the architecture
> Of the whole in a haze of suppressed mockery,
> Are beside the point.
>
> (484)

This attack on critics of the system berates critics specifically for trying to "invest" with "aura" that which has been stripped of it, to find a vantage exterior to the system so as to mock it, call it by its name. Ashbery's uncharacteristic anger here seems an index to his insistence that we are after aura, that there is no exterior, and that trying to crawl back into the art of the past, as it were, is delusional:

This could have been our paradise: exotic
Refuge within an exhausted world, but that wasn't
In the cards, because it wouldn't have been
The point.

(487)

But what is this "play," this pseudolife, better than? What *is* "the point"? As Ashbery winds up the poem, he suggests that englobed existence is better, at least, than universal violence:

It seems like a very hostile universe
But as the principle of each individual thing is
Hostile to, exists at the expense of all the others
As philosophers have often pointed out, at least
This thing, the mute, undivided present,
Has the justification of logic, which
In this instance isn't a bad thing

(485)

The "logic" here seems to be a logic by which flooding time with continuous event displaces differences among things that, in punctual time, would war endlessly with each other. This Hobbesianism is very different from the tenor of Ashbery's work, with its emphasis on Heraclitean flux. Indeed, as I have been arguing, the whole movement of the first part of the book is to offer the fluid, over and over, against the punctual as a model for livable relation to time. What has happened? Has the discovery, in a sixteenth-century painting, of the dark work in fluidity disqualified it, *tout court*, from offering the poet any consolation in the face of apocalypse, or "an exhausted world"? Are the arbitrary consolations of the first part of the book really worse than the resignation that greets the discovery that flux has a social as well as a natural dimension? Does Ashbery really think that these are the terms of the choice he faces? He alters his course:

at least
This thing, the mute, undivided present,
Has the justification of logic, which
In this instance isn't a bad thing
Or wouldn't be, if the way of telling
Didn't somehow intrude, twisting the end result
Into a caricature of itself. This always

Happens, as in the game where
A whispered phrase passed around the room
Ends up something completely different.

(485)

This twisting "way of telling," Ashbery adds, "is the principle that makes the work of art so unlike / What the artist intended." Language, then, both spoken language and artistic language, flies in the face of the would-be "logic" by which a magma of pseudo-event is preferable to universal violence. Something in his own medium prevents him from making the one preferable to the other.

Because we know that the poet experiences Parmigianino's painting, not as a false work of art, then, but as a carrier of actual pathos, we need to understand a little better the significance of the painter's technical achievement mirroring so closely the chilling operation of the self-demonstrating society, the magical sum. And a small door opens for us when Ashbery claims that there is something *about language* that makes it impossible to narrate the work of the system, the system whose distortions mimic language's. That door opens on to the possibility that englobed existence looks so much like reality, not because it is "natural" in the same sense as language is, but because the work of the system captures and makes use of something in language. In poems like "Grand Galop," Ashbery fretted over the ways in which a baffling division of labor meant that he would never, by himself, understand the histories into which he'd been inserted, "forced to fret over insufficient details related to huge / Unfinished concepts"; here, near the end of the poem, he laments,

Each person
Has one big theory to explain the universe
But it doesn't tell the whole story
And in the end it is what is outside him
That matters, to him and especially to us

(486)

The painful division of conceptual work and aesthetic experience that leads Ashbery to bid farewell to Parmigianino and his painting is in fact a farewell to aesthetic experience itself. No theory will bring it back: the work of enclosure has so successfully captured the linguistic processes it imitates that even the landscape seems to imitate the system, rather than the other way around:

One feels too confined,
Sifting the April sunlight for clues,
In the mere stillness of the ease of its
Parameter

(487)

The painter falls away; the poet, on the porch of the englobed city ("it is the gibbous / mirrored eye of an insect"), prepares for a similar fate. His account of aesthetic experience began with the guilty relief of discovering that time stuffed full of event, though sometimes painful to the senses, allowed the subject to walk away from disasters experienced more brutally elsewhere. He ends with an aesthetic endgame, the freeze-dried Proustianism of "cold pockets / Of remembrance," and a lament that no theory of aesthetic experience can bridge the divides among "us."

What seems needed is not so much a theory of the aesthetic, however, as a theory of language—at least, that is, if it is the procedures of language that the spectacle battens on to in order to simulate life, to fake freedom. Ashbery is not the poet of such theories; but some of his contemporaries, especially on the West Coast, were interested in language theory, rather than aesthetic theory, for exactly the reasons I have been outlining here. Ashbery's truly probing account of the aesthetic, in the 1970s, meets with a violence that eludes naming. For the poets of "language," the problem needed to be reframed.

— 3 —
"Language" in Spicer and After

This chapter traces the local byways of a "turn to language" in one influential poetic subculture of the 1950s and 1960s, the scene of the Berkeley and San Francisco "renaissances." It also outlines the appropriation and reworking of this linguistic turn in the Language poets of the 1970s and 1980s. The overall movement of my argument is to suggest that this turn to an idea of poems as events in language, rather than as aesthetic objects, is developed as a response to the new forms of spectacularization, commodification, and enclosure that took hold in San Francisco at midcentury. My focus in the first part of this chapter is on the meanings of "language" generated by the poet Jack Spicer, and how they give rise to an idea about the social function of poetic form, which is to hide and protect forms of experience that are endangered by the encroachments of capital on subcultural life.[1]

Spicer's sense of the endangerment of poetry aligns him in certain ways with Ashbery. Both of them were grounded in urban gay subcultural scenes, and both developed a sense of poetry as a minor art, requiring camouflage and dispersal to survive. But Ashbery's sense of poetic minority is built around an insistence on its harmlessness, while Spicer's is built out of a militant insistence on the strict boundaries around coterie relations. And the gesture that permits Ashbery to keep writing, his looking or wandering away from crisis, produces a very different textual environment than does the key gesture in Spicer's poetry, which is more like a slap, a flourish, or a card trick. Ashbery wants to avoid crisis, or to make it disappear by ignoring it; Spicer wants to be vigilantly alert to crisis, almost seeming at times to want to trigger it. Ashbery has always demurred from identifying as a "gay poet"; Spicer wrote short poetic essays called "Homosexuality and Marxism" and worked with the Mattachine Society in Oakland on a midcentury "gay agenda" (Killian, "Spicer and the Mattachine"). Ashbery's New York is the city of traffic, whose glory and danger is the rapidity of its material accumulation; Spicer's San Francisco is the city of earthquakes, whose allure and threat rest on its hair-trigger location.

Another difference between the two poets, and the one that will shape this chapter, has to do with poetic program. Ashbery, in his affiliation with a minor "tradition," is always and clearly dead-set against the idea of establishing criteria for poetic value in advance of any given poem. But Spicer, more than any other poet in this study besides Pound, experienced poetry as needing some kind of program or set of guidelines for practitioners. His sense of what such a guide or program might be was not, as with Pound, elaborated in any critical writing; it emerges, instead, scattered among the poems themselves, and in the record of his coterie relationships with friends and disciples. For this reason I read Spicer from a variety of angles, focusing in turn on his ideas about seriality, rhetorical invention, noise and spectacle, the function of legend, and the usefulness of shock. Each of these contributes to a poetic program aimed at protecting poetry—from mass culture, from capital—and preserving its specificity, both as a historical relation to language and as a social practice.

Seriality and Fragment

For Spicer, no single poem can fully inhabit or realize the category of "poetry." In a letter to the poet Robin Blaser, included as part of the 1958 volume *Admonitions,* he puts it this way:

> The trick naturally is what Duncan learned years ago and tried to teach us—not to search for the perfect poem but to let your way of writing of the moment go along its own paths, explore and retreat but never fully be realized (confined) within the boundaries of one poem . . . [Duncan said there was no good or bad poetry.] There is—but not in relation to a single poem. There is really no single poem. (*Collected Poetry,* 163)

Spicer remained true to this notion of the single poem as only part of an ongoing "writing" or "poetry" no single poem can realize. It is why, ten years after Spicer's death in 1965, the poet Peter Riley could say of Spicer's work, "I think that a concept of total reading has to come into play, by which the poem is a transfer of action to the reader's imaginal field" ("Narratives of the Holy Grail," 167). "Total reading," here, emerges from exactly the condition of each single poem only partly realizing the concept of "poetry"; oddly, this partial realization itself is a result of each poem, ideally at least, being what Riley calls "absolutely complete"—each poem, that is, must strive as best as it can to achieve participation in the forming of the concept of poetry. So there is a strange relationship of unrealizability between parts—none of which is aesthetically "perfect"—and their ability to feel "complete" against the backdrop of a totality of poetry that takes its place in some kind of "field."

Spicer phrased and rephrased his own ideas about parts and wholes many times in his own writing. In a poem called "A Textbook of Poetry," he puts it this way:

> It does not have to fit together. Like the pieces of a
> totally unfinished jigsaw puzzle my grandmother left in the
> bedroom when she died in the living room. The pieces of the
> poetry or of this love.
>
> (Collected Poetry, 299)

Elsewhere, in a series called "Phonemics," he writes, "Empty fragments, like the shards of pots found in some Mesopotamian expedition. Found but not put together" (393). We are very far, though, from an Eliotic sense of fragments shored against ruin. Spicer does have a sense of civilizational crisis, but it is not built around a melancholic differentiation between a past classical heritage and a modern disarray. Spicer's sense of crisis has more to do with something like what we would now call globalization—a crisis of the local felt as the encroachments of the global, a crisis in which the pleasures of nonsense, of what can be made out of the gaps between "pieces of poetry" or "shards of pots," will be sealed over by television, by mass culture, by the nationalization of a literary "business" at odds with the local conditions of the production of literature. In this sense Spicer is closer to Ashbery—it is the emulsification and becoming indifferent to what came before, rather than its shattering, that Spicer dreads. This is because for him, poetic language is enlivened by what seeps into it between the gaps it leaves open: fragmentation is necessary, not because the fragment has a self-evident or ironic pathos, but because language lives off the transmutation of nonlanguage, of nonsense, into language.

Spicer, then, is neither a high modernist nor a romantic in his interest in the fragment. He is something more like a hybrid of poetic linguist and romantic philologist, using poetry to discern the boundaries and the texture of the medium of language, and using his sense of language as a specific medium to piece together a holistic sense of the special character of "poetry." Indeed, Spicer worked in the linguistics department at the University of California, Berkeley, from 1958 to 1964, teaching classes and helping Professor David Reed research West Coast dialect speech. He also studied as an undergraduate at Berkeley with the medieval historian Ernst Kantorowicz, who seems to have helped Spicer form a sense of poetry as part of a shifting corpus of textual matter with overlapping and different versions of the same story, like the different versions of the Arthur legend that compose the multilingual "Matter of Britain," or the variations of detail that mark different versions of songs in the ballad tradition (Ellingham and Killian 19–21, 122). A poetic fragment, then, has for Spicer the dual charge of being an event in language, and a piece of something like literary "matter," part of a set of concerns and topics. These settings for poetry are kept fresh and alive by variation, substitution, and the transformation of nonsense into language, by a whole variety of activities Spicer called—almost certainly knowing the rhetorical sense of his word choice—"invention."

Enclosure and Counterenclosure

Spicer's linguistic-philological sense of the specificity of poetry has one other important parameter, one that is specific to the San Francisco literary scene of the late 1950s and early 1960s. For Spicer, poetry, permeable though it needs to be to the nonpoetic, works as a kind of counterenclosure to the encroachments of mass culture, the culture of business, and the enlarged scale of violence after the world wars. Spicer's biographers Lewis Ellingham and Kevin Killian write of the poet being terrified of the possibility of a Russian invasion during the Cuban Missile Crisis in 1962, to the point of advising friends to start saving water; they also recount his disgust with the music of the Beatles, whose songs began to displace the kind of noise Spicer and his crowd liked to generate in the bars of North Beach. Where Spicer and his friends had once instigated a popular "Blabbermouth Night," in which patrons were urged on to ever-greater feats of spontaneous hyperbole and nonsense, by 1962 the North Beach bars were ever friendlier to that music Spicer called "devoid of form and color, but full of images" (Ellingham and Killian 255, 306, 99–100).

It sounds like a good early description of white noise—and, for that matter, of the spectacle as Guy Debord anatomized it. This is to say that for

Spicer the local disruptions of texture and rhythm caused by mass culture had high stakes—they were linked, in his mind, to vaster forms of violence and to more insidious kinds of enclosure. In an untitled poem from the 1964 sequence "Thing Language," Spicer writes:

> I
> Can-
> not
> accord
> sympathy
> to
> those who
> do
> not
> recognize
> The human crisis.

A few lines before, he explains:

> We give equal
> Space to everything in our lives. Eich-
> Mann proved that false in killing like you raise wildflowers.
>   Witlessly
>
> (379)

The mass murder of European Jews "proves" to the poet that space, that accommodation, is not made for "everything in our lives," that some "things" crowd out others, much as "the human crisis," on the page, is crowding out the poem, from right to left.

Other spatial figures for obliteration or for crowding out mark the poems from "Thing Language":

> A redwood forest is not invisible at night. The blackness covers it but it covers the blackness.
>
> If they had turned Jeffers into a parking lot death would have been eliminated and birth also. The lights shine 24 hours a day on a parking lot.
>
> True conservation is the effort of the artist and the private man to keep things true. Trees and the cliffs in Big Sur breathe in the dark. Jeffers knew the pain of their

> breath and the pain was the death of a first-born baby
> breathing.
>   Death is not final. Only parking lots.
>
> (377)

Worse than death, then, because it disrupts a rhythm of life and death naturalized here as breathing, is 24-hour-a-day illumination, which doubles the covering-over of earth by pavement by covering over darkness. The poet's place in this horror, indexed by the fantasy of the poet Robinson Jeffers mismemorialized into pavement, is to "keep things true," which seems to mean to keep them mortal.

As for those in Spicer's circle who saw no harm in dancing to "A Hard Day's Night," or who wanted to participate in the pleasures of mass culture, which Spicer saw as a pseudolife—well, it was for these people that Spicer could not "accord / sympathy." He kept a cordon separating those who did and those who didn't resist the 24-hour glare of the emergent spectacle and what he saw as its link to mass violence. Anyone could cross over, if they proved true to his sense of poetry as more than aesthetic, but he did not hold back from denouncing those who lingered on the other side.

Spicer's companions resisted what they saw as his tests of loyalty, even as they admired his will to purity in writing. The record of their skirmishes is considerable; here is a piece of correspondence between Spicer and the younger writer Stan Persky, who published Spicer in his North Beach magazine, *Open Space*. Spicer writes across town to the magazine:

> July 30, 1964
>
> Dear Stan Persky (I add the last name because I am sick of the tea-party first name business, my fault as well as yours, as if Open Space were a Turkish Bath of the imagination):
>
> The only poem that interested me in the whole July issue (including my own) was the rhymed poem called "Underwier" about half-way through the issue. Though the signature of it is given as Lew Ellingham, he tells me that the authors, in tandem, were you, Ron Primack, and Jim Alexander. The poem seems to me better than anything the three of you have written in the last two years and I wonder why you did not give your names to it.
>
> Something happened. It isn't happening often enough now and I wonder if the accusation against Open Space is not that it is too homosexual but that it is too homogeneous. Like cartons of milk.
>
> . . .

> I am, nonetheless, submitting poems in this August issue and will continue to even if things get worse.
>
> Sincerely yours,
>
> Jack Spicer

Persky replies:

> Dear Jack,
>
> This is the last "Open Space"—like the end of part one; but not the end of the magazine—because as a poet my business is to do what's really real. The only point where you and I agree now is that people don't read poetry; hardly anymore.
>
> Trying to figure out . . . how to be fair [to you] is hard, who have so often used unfairness for your way. Even in my dreams you confuse me by two of you: Dirty Jack and Radiant Jack. In one part I come into your room, your back to me, I see your elbows in the holes of your shirt, the oily glass, the back of you looms up big as a ship, and you growl and tell me to give it up. In Radiant Jack you yourself come to the warehouse where we're working, wearing clean sports-clothes, and you have tickets to the ballgame for me. It isn't that you've given little or withheld too much . . . but it seems to me you want a world small enough so that wherever you spit you'll hit something, a world you can control. (Ellingham and Killian 302–303)

Spicer's praise of the uncredited collaboration among Persky, Primack, and Alexander is the obverse of his impatience with what he sees as the milk-carton homogeneity of the rest of the poetry in *Open Space:* the countercondition to commodity-like homogeneity is the mixing of poetic egos. But he wants the collaboration signed—as with his insistence on using last names in his correspondence, he wants to restore to his literary relationships a sense that they take place *in print,* the medium of writers. At first glance Spicer seems to link this print mixedness to the ideal of a specifically heterosexual scene of poetic community: he uses two figures of same-sex sociability, the ladies' "tea-party" and the men's "Turkish Bath," to describe the thinness of the poetry he dislikes. But Spicer has a problem with homogeneity, not homosexuality, and he is not advocating heterosexuality but a heterogeneity—instanced as authorial mixing—that militates against a sameness figured, not as homosexuality, but as careless, chummy homosociality.[2]

At the time of this exchange, Spicer was 39, Persky 23; the younger writer both mimics Spicer's poetic stance and struggles to critique its implications. On the one hand Persky precisely imitates Spicer's equation of serial form with poetic authenticity. He links the nonfinal character of the last issue of *Open Space* ("like the end of part one—but not the end of the magazine") with his commitment "as a poet" to do what's "really real," that is, to locate authenticity not in any one literary organ but in commitment to the category of "poetry" itself. On the other hand, Persky senses that Spicer's resistance to the commodification of poetry, to its becoming homogeneous like "cartons of milk," has resulted in its own form of enclosure, "a world small enough that wherever you'll spit you'll hit something." Persky cannot experience the two practices—the serial quest for poetic purity, with its alluring integrity, and the stern, even cruel, rejection of friendliness, with its concomitant enclosure, its cordoned-off "world"—as coming from the same person: hence "Dirty Jack" and "Radiant Jack." But the two men of the dream—the grubby, cruel, impoverished one, and the fresh, flush, generous one—are both bound up in what Persky renders as "the warehouse," the scene of shared poetic labor that Spicer is willing to picket, as it were, if it threatens to produce commodities instead of poems.[3] The young Persky senses the tension at the heart of Spicer's work, or its greatest challenge: it is a poetics of social relation, which implies at every turn that social relations must be managed as part of the poetic process. Spicer envisions that management as the keeping of his cohort clear of the market, but his friends experience it as volatile and bivalent, both a form of integrity and an intimidating move toward cultlike fixity. The correspondence and the biography demonstrate that the poets around Spicer felt a constant tension between the world-making possibilities of the poem, as Spicer expounded on it, and the world-enclosing strategies meant to protect "poetry."

The ambivalence is everywhere. Ellingham and Killian meticulously track endless quarrels and feuds between Spicer and his circle, and quote Duncan referring to Spicer's desire for a "Kreis"—a cultic formation of admirers along the lines of the cryptohomosexual circle around Stefan George in Weimar Germany. But they also cite George Stanley saying, "If Spicer thought your poem was shit, that didn't mean he thought you were shit," and the records of Spicer's correspondence show both the poet and his interlocutors signing even very vituperative letters "love" (*Poet Be Like God,* 181, 116).[4] It's as though he made use of the same serial model for his friendships as he did with his poetry: no one exchange, no one moment of friendship, could be expected to be perfect; it was the whole, the quest even, that mattered. And he made his cohort feel this. The young poet Dora Geissler, describing the height of the bar-centered scene around Spicer, recalls a sense that "the whole was so much greater than its parts, so that when we left the group, we felt so diminished that we couldn't bear to separate from each other" (146).

"The pieces of the poetry or of this love": the scene around Spicer left a striking record of the struggle of one milieu to achieve a kind of counter-totality to the one emerging after the Second World War. The sense among Spicer's poetic friends of being part of a "whole" that was "greater than it parts" was both his social and his poetic aim. It was a strain on the people who participated in it, but the poems Spicer was writing clearly made trying well worth their while. So what was in those poems? What was their social magic?

Invention and Magic

My best sense of the specialness of Spicer's poetry, its allure, has to do with how the poet used the techniques of substitution, rearrangement, and surprise that grew out of his commitment to serial forms. An older rhetoric would group the strategies Spicer developed for his poems under the headings of invention and disposition—the creation of subject matter, and the arrangement of its parts. And these older terms do a certain degree of justice to the excitement of reading the poems, especially when Spicer asks us to think of poetry as partaking in a kind of transmutation, or as having a certain kind of essence. But I should make clear that it's the historical situation Spicer imagines himself in, as much as any magic of *inventio* or *dispositio,* that gives the poems their charge. Or: it's the meeting of the situation with the strategies. In the broadest sense, though, what I want to draw attention to is how the poem, as part of a series, is a kind of laboratory, an enclosed but permeable space for the creation of the new. I want to walk through one instance of how such poems work, and to do it in detail, in the service of linking Spicer's technique to the larger social project I have been describing.

Take the well-known poem "Sporting Life," part of Spicer's 1964 volume *Thing Language*:

> The trouble with comparing a poet with a radio is that radios
>   don't develop scar-tissue. The tubes burn out, or with a

> transistor, which most souls are, the battery or diagram
> burns out replaceable or not replaceable, but not like that
> punchdrunk fighter in the bar. The poet
> Takes too many messages. The right to the ear that floored
> him
> in New Jersey. The right to say that he stood six rounds
> with a champion.
> Then they sell beer or go on sporting commissions, or, if the
> scar tissue is too heavy, demonstrate in a bar where the
> invisible champions might not have hit him. Too many of
> them.
> The poet is a radio. The poet is a liar. The poet is a
> counterpunching radio.
> And those messages (God would not damn them) do not even
> know they are champions.
>
> (373–374)

The poem, though plainspoken, plays a complicated little game of transpositions, options, and recursions. It begins with undermining one of Spicer's own favorite comparisons, poet-as-radio, on grounds—scar tissue—that the metaphor can't hold because of an organic–inorganic difference between its two parts. But he reinstates it and branches it out in the next sentence, "the tubes burn out, or with a transistor, which most souls are, the battery or diagram burns out." These two divisions of the freshly restored poet-radio metaphor—tube and battery-or-diagram—are casually interrupted by "which most souls are," a phrase that upends the significance of "souls" to the body, and to the metaphor, by locating it off to the side, between commas. The sentence continues with a subdivision of the transistor-tubes half of his figure, "replaceable or not replaceable," and then, having established a comic punctiliousness about this metaphor from which he inaugurally disinvested himself, he returns to the disinvestment, while further specifying that the poet is not like a radio: "but not like that punchdrunk fighter in the bar." The "that," which actually introduces the figure of the "punchdrunk fighter," behaves as though he has been on the scene of the poem already. Abruptly, we are in a new structure, poet-as-not-radio-but-boxer-though-sort-of-still-radio. Spicer elaborates: "the poet/Takes too many messages," the overload implicitly the reason for the "scar tissue," and the "messages" are themselves split into two kinds, first as the unimpeachable delivery of a punch—"the right to the ear that floored him / in New Jersey," then as a pun on the punch, "the right to say that he stood six rounds / with a champion."

This nearly Ramist exfoliation of laterality is followed with the briefest of storylines, the story of the fighter past his prime, trying to retool himself from a commodity into a salesman, or into a legend:

> Then they sell beer or go on sporting commissions, or, if the
> scar tissue is too heavy, demonstrate in a bar where the
> invisible champions might not have hit him. Too many of
> them.

Even the story has an either-or structure, though, here hinging not on the existence but on the thickness of the "scar tissue," which determines whether the aging fighter can make a living or just hang out and drink. In the latter case, it seems, he tends to untruth, pointing out the places on his body "where the invisible champions might not have hit him." The next sentence, "Too many of them," is built to hover: too many punches, too many champions, too many hits to be believed.

It is also something like the climax of the poem, which now turns to a rapid-fire conclusion whose speed is derived from its ready access the number of options in the air:

> The poet is a radio. The poet is a liar. The poet is a
> counterpunching radio.
> And those messages (God would not damn them) do not even
> know they are champions.

"The poet is a radio" swipes back at the poem's first claim, even though its credibility is damaged; "The poet is a liar" lands harder, because the evidence has mounted for it, at least if we consider that the aging fighter is a figure for the poet. And if we prefer the clever negativity of thinking of the poet as "the poet," lying to us right here, in situ, then the next sentence in the 1–2–3, "The poet is a / counterpunching radio," packs the biggest wallop, not only for how it fuses the organic and the inorganic that were separated at the poem's outset, but for how it suddenly makes poetry a minor kind of radio, hitting back at "major" radio, the real radio that would drown it out. The last sentence eulogizes the "messages" that were punches but now are counterpunches, calling them "champions" though they cannot themselves "know" it, perhaps because they work in a more anonymous medium, perhaps because they are more like scar tissue than owned or rented AM-FM frequency, and don't have the luxury of being everywhere and nowhere, invulnerable. The god who appears in parentheses, forgivingly, before the poem concludes, signals that the poet knows he has a little extra time before he lands his last blow, that he can afford a late aside on God to match his earlier aside on the soul, because the poem's readers are still dazed, trying to assimilate its texture of comparisons—bifurcated and retracted, negated and revived. So what if poets lie?

I think the key to the thrill of "Sporting Life" is its late acceleration, which I always experience as akin to the speed picked up at the end of a sestina, when the six end-words of the first six six-line stanzas are recycled in only three lines in the poem's final tercet. That halving of the stanza length while keeping all six words in play is a bit like what Spicer manages above, returning at the end to "poet," "radio," "messages," and "champions," while revising one of them ("counterpunching") and adding a fifth ("liar"). This recombination, along with the introduction of "liar," gives the close of the poem an alchemical feel, as though "liar" were distilled out of the reordering of the other four words, though with a sheen or altered valence derived from the lies being forgiven, even being understood as the source of triumph (as part of what makes the messages poets hear "champions"). The poem is both self-enclosed and open, recombinant and inductive—taking up "lying," for instance, and returning it to the world reused. It feels like a fabulous card trick. But the poem has done more than dazzle: it has reinvented the ancient reply to the ancient accusation against poets by situating their "lies" in the barroom, where not lies, but legends, are made.[5]

Legend and Camouflage

I have suggested that for Spicer the recombinant and inductive magic of disposition and invention is a poem-level technique for participating in the testing of the boundaries of poetic language, and for staging the poem as a porous but enclosed language laboratory, which always points, serially, to the category "poetry." I have also argued that Spicer deploys this serial model of poems and poetry, instance and category, as a way of organizing both his poetics and the poetry scene against homogenization and commodification, which he sees as linked to the pseudolife of the emergent spectacle, and to the mass violence of midcentury. Finally, I suggested earlier that Spicer's sense of the category "poetry" is modeled on a cross between how he imagines the body of the ballad tradition and the romance narrative to have emerged, and his sense of poetry as an event in the medium of language. Legend has a special function in this context.

To read Spicer's collected books is to be struck with the consistency of his interest in legend and its significance as a transtextual medium for poems. In book after book, sequence after sequence, Spicer makes use of the conceit that he is merely visiting a preexisting corpus in order to work changes on it. This poetic strategy is extremely generative for Spicer, both in terms of individual poems, which take advantage of the conceit in order to heighten the inventive variability I detailed above, and in terms of Spicer's poetics, because staging himself as visitor to a preexisting textual corpus or "matter" allows him to present "poetry" as passing through, but not limited to, individual poems.

Spicer makes use of many versions of this strategy. *After Lorca* (1957) is full of unscored "ballads" dedicated to other writers; *A Book of Music* (1958) is subtitled "with words by Jack Spicer," as though the poems—which are not set to music—were merely secondarily fixed onto a preexisting body of song; the short sequence *Billy the Kid* (1958) riffs on what kind of substantiality a figure from legend can have; "A Fake Novel about the Life of Arthur Rimbaud," part of the book *The Heads of the Town Up to the Aether* (1961), places Rimbaud in a kind of counterfactual historical fantasia that Spicer calls "the lives of Rimbaud"; and *The Holy Grail* (1962) takes up the "matter of Britain" from the perspectives of seven of its protagonists, each of whom skeptically remarks on the ever-shifting meaning of the grail. These are all playful conceits: none of the "ballads" resemble traditional ballad form, and none of the material from the medieval romance follows the sequence of the legend. But the local strategies of invention and disposition that I detailed in "Sporting Life" take on particular resonance when we read them as Spicer's attempt to reproduce, in individual poems, the kinds of versioning he sees making up the material body of "poetry"—a body composed of variant textual instances whose distribution in space and time keeps the category breathing.

In *Billy the Kid,* legend is figured as interstitial to the larger category poetry, which operates as a field or medium in which legendary content can be stashed away:

> The radio that day told me about the death of Billy The Kid
> (And the day, a hot summer day, with birds in the sky)

> Let us fake out a frontier—a poem somebody could hide in with a sheriff's posse after him—
>
> (185)

The faked-out "frontier" is something like the poem-as-medium, wherein is stashed the substance of legend. This language is akin to the redwood forest in "Thing Language," breathing in the dark, protected by darkness from the 24-hour glare of the new sprawl. It is also a bit paranoid, and I'm sorry to say that as a form of counterenclosure, the poetics of stashed-away legendary essence carries with it some ugliness—not least the anti-Semitism of the lines "a poem with no hard corners, no houses to get lost in, no underwebbing of customary magic, no New York Jew salesmen of amethyst pajamas." The turning of the fantasy of renegade nomadism, uncaptured by domicile, by custom, or by exchange, into a cheap shot at Jews is deflating to say the least.[6] I am going to press ahead, though, because I think Spicer's notion of poetic matter is important enough to investigate in detail.

Spicer's idea of poetry as camouflaging legendary content modulates in *Billy the Kid* into a language of "shadows," of hiding in the shade, where Billy's shadow is "carefully/distinguished from all of [the other] shadows"—distinct, but still safe from scrutiny. This shadow language mixes with a language of indiscernibility, of indifference, as though gradations of shade or darkness facilitated a meditation on sameness, on essence even:

> So the heart breaks
> Into small shadows
> Almost so random
> They are meaningless
> Like a diamond
> Has at the center of it a diamond
> Or a rock
> Rock.

This atomic sameness becomes the language of love as arriving-at-meaninglessness, in which the poet becomes nothing more than a constituent feature of the Billy legend, a drop of his essence:

> Billy The Kid
> I love you

Billy The Kid
I back anything you say[7]

(191)

Later, in his book series *Lament for the Makers* (1961), Spicer revisits this matrix of dead legendary figure, erotic compulsion, and stashing-away or hiddenness in an anecdote about the corpse of D. H. Lawrence:

> "Then Frieda [Lawrence, the writer's wife] told us an incredible story. Someone who wanted Lawrence—and Frieda named the possessive admirer—wanted him in death as well as in life. Frieda's house was invaded and Lawrence's ashes were stolen.
>
> 'You can believe,' said Frieda, 'I had a hard time getting them back. But I recovered them. And I made up my mind that nothing of the sort should happen again. So I fixed it.'
>
> 'How?' we asked. 'What did you do?'
>
> 'I had the ashes mixed with a lot of sand and concrete. Now they are in a huge concrete slab. It weighs over a ton.' She laughed heartily. 'A dozen men could not lift it.'" (322)

There is probably no more illuminating parable in the Spicer corpus than this one for bringing together the forms of mixedness that excited the poet in the coauthored poem in Persky's magazine *Open Space,* the hiddenness that facilitates erotic union in *Billy the Kid,* and the sense of poetry needing a betweenness that Spicer fears will be paved over in his poem on Robinson Jeffers's mismemorialization as a parking lot. You can see it's not concrete or pavement per se that's good or bad, in Spicer's mind: it serves a horrible deathless covering-over in the poem on Jeffers, but is a witty medium for preservation in the Lawrence anecdote. What's important for Spicer is to argue for the nonhomogeneity of media, for preserving and nurturing their mixedness—which is crucial, Spicer believes, to keeping at bay the overzealous, the possessive.

So Spicer depicts poetry as a medium—a field, a frontier—in which the erotically charged content of legend can be hidden and protected. But it is also true that Spicer figures poetry as that which needs protection, and elsewhere in his work he stashes in it the larger "field" of language, much in the way that legend is tucked into the interstices of poetry, above.

Shock and Transformation

In a sequence called "Transformations," from the serial poem *Language* (1964), Spicer both distinguishes and blends the poetic and the linguistic:

TRANSFORMATIONS II
"In Scarlet Town where I was born
There was a fair maid dwelling."
We make up a different language for poetry
And for the heart—ungrammatical.
It is not that the name of the town changes
(Scarlet becomes Charlotte or even in Gold City I once heard
 a good Western singer make it Tonapah. We don't have towns
 here)
(That sort of thing would please the Jungian astronauts)
But that the syntax changes. This is older than towns.
Troy was a baby when Greek sentence structure emerged. This
 was the real Trojan Horse.
The order changes. The Trojans
Having no idea of true or false syntax and having no recorded
 language
Never knew what hit them.

(390)

I read the poem as aligning "poetry and the heart," on the one hand, and the body of the ballad tradition, on the other. Here the shifting versions of "Barbara Allen," which Spicer sees as semantic, are contrasted with the "ungrammatical" shifts in "poetry and the heart"—a romantic problem that is romantically reworked, in the poem, as the Trojan War—as with the poetry of the "counterpunching radio," here the Trojans "never knew what hit them."

Despite the historical analogy, Spicer sees these "transformations" as part of the dailiness of language—indeed, he is working the title of this sequence to reflect a linguistic understanding of "transformation" as the operation by which languages allow speakers to move between passive and active phrasings of a sentence, or between declarative and interrogative arrangements of semantic content.[8] This is clear in the first poem of the sequence, where transformation is analogized to point of view, given a range of emotion, and even a kind of politics:

TRANSFORMATIONS I
They say "he need (plural) enemy (plural)"
I am not them. This is the first transformation.
They say "we need (present) no enemy (singular)" No enemy in the
universe is theirs worth having. We is an intimate pronoun which
shifts its context almost as the I blinks at it. Those
Swans we saw in the garden coming out of the water we hated them.
"Out of place," you said in passing. Those swans and I (a blink in
context), all out of place we hated you.
He need (present) enemy (plural) and now it is the swans and me
against you
Everything out of place
(And now another blink of moment) the last swan back in place. We
Hated them.

(389)

Instead of Greeks and Trojans, here two friends or lovers align and unalign themselves across the line of the question of what's "out of place," what belongs. At the same time the poet first dissociates himself from the "they," presumably the linguists who transcribe sentences using parentheses to note verb tenses or numbers of objects—"I am not them"—only to make use of their method of transcription in the poem's fourth strophe. The poem seizes on the idea of a "transformation" as a grammatical shift, then alters the idea so as to give situational content to what is first rendered as professional form: "he need (plural) enemy (plural)." "Transformation" becomes a question of the "I" being or not being "them," as well as a question of what is or isn't "out of place," which seems to determine the line between "hatred" and the "intimacy" of the first-person plural.

It bears emphasizing, here, that the poem shifts between linguistic and poetic senses of "transformation." The two senses of the word share, for Spicer, a distinction between the semantic and the syntactical, but in the poetic case Spicer seizes on the semantic content in order to ring syntactical changes on it. The content does matter, it *is* matter—but it only becomes interesting, poetic, by way of rearrangements of perspective and subject-object priority. Poetry is "ungrammatical" in the somewhat confusing sense that it derives significance not from varying content but by deforming it, by ringing changes on the structure that houses it. This is both very "grammatical" in its distinction between structure and content and very rhetorical in its respect for content as the trigger for structure: the "Barbara Allen" ballad and "he need (plural) enemy (plural)" are more than incidental to Spicer, though he wants to resituate them. To return to my shell-game analogy, the content of a ballad, as the poet positions and repositions it before our eyes, is not so much analogous to what is hidden under one of the shells as to the shells themselves—which themselves house another "content" that, though it is given shape by what lies under the winning shell, is really the content of the game: player and played.

Even at the level of the "linguistic," then, for Spicer poetry is about the social relationships it helps induce, or that induce it. Perhaps this is why Spicer's 1957 poetry workshop at the San Francisco Public Library was called "Poetry as Magic"; and why Helen Adam, one of the workshop's key members, wrote a play about it on the model of a quest narrative, in which an initiate seeks entrance into the realm of the working poets.[9] For Spicer the poet is a kind of trickster-teacher, gaming initiates so as to make them see what isn't exactly there—a poetry between the lines, as it were. He even teaches this "magic" to toddlers: his friend Jim Herndon recalls Spicer's relationship with his 3-year-old son Jay, and how Spicer would tell the boy that the real name for his unwanted potatoes and broccoli was "Child Psychology," or roar, when he left the Herndon's apartment at the end of the night, that he was "Goin' to Texas!" As Herndon puts it:

> Children ought to be told a random combination of fantasy, outright lies and simple truth, all in the same tone of voice. The Giant's Garden, pigs can fly, cows eat grass. Correctly applied, this principle would keep the child's mind inviolate, curious, alert, and above all, wary. (*Manroot* 10, 1974–1975, 57)

Herndon recalls this notion of pedagogy being political for Spicer, that it could serve as an antidote to pieties in the teaching of American history, so full of myth. Much later, the poet and critic Bruce Boone would write about Spicer's insistence on the mixing—and the mixedness—of truth and untruth, "The real and fake only make sense in terms of some always-seeming-to-be-impending disaster. You better be careful, is Spicer's advice—you might miss the point if you [aren't]" ("For Jack Spicer," 120).

Boone's remark deftly identifies the "fakery" in Spicer as a strategy for dealing with a kind of "disaster" with a funny temporality, carefully marked as "always-seeming-to-be-impending." I don't think Boone is trying to distance himself from Spicer by including "seeming" in his description; I think he is trying to identify the dark magic of the spectacle itself, which exposes itself periodically as requiring violence, before subsiding into a condition of "normalcy." "Always-seeming-to-be-impending" could be a description of paranoid interpretive practices, certainly, but it is actually more accurate as a description of the absorption of mass violence in the buffered industrial North, which both senses the implications of violence elsewhere in the world but is easily distracted from those implications in the onrush of new sensation released, not by mass violence, but by the provisional safety and the distraction it keeps funding for those protected from it.

Eichmann; paved-over parking lots; the displacement of bar culture and balladeering by the Beatles: the leaps of scale required to see each of these as linked can be difficult to make, can indeed seem like a kind of paranoid or arbitrary reading practice. Or they can become part of a scale-jumping poetic reading practice, where "disaster" peers in through the poem's interstices, and shocks the poem:

> Smoke signals
> Like in the Eskimo villages on the coast where the earthquake
>   hit
> Bang, snap, crack. They will never know what hit them
> On the coast of Alaska. They expect everybody to be insane.
> This is a poem about the death of John F. Kennedy.
>
> (377)

Like the Trojans sprung upon by Greek syntax, the Eskimos "will never know what hit them"—or, like the punchdrunk boxer, years after his prime, the poet will have to reconstruct what hit him, stage it again so its force can be felt afresh. As usual, we readers are included in the dynamic of being startled: how is the poem about JFK exactly? It takes an extra beat to answer that question with, we-never-knew-what-hit-us-either.

If each poem, for Spicer, serially indexes the category poetry, it also points to crisis—each poem stages forms of swiftness and distraction designed to land a blow that is a kind of "counterpunch" to the "the human crisis" that is so easy to ignore, or to miss. The strategies I have detailed here, of rhetorical invention and arrangement, of the analogy to linguistics, the analogy to literary matter—all of these are ways of situating poetry in a "matter" or a medium so as to present the poem as an *event*—especially an event between reader and writer, but also between lover and beloved, teacher and initiate, friend and friend.

So totality and coterie are wound together, stratagem and sociability, to make the poem confront a crisis, and to stash away a kind of magic made to ward it off. It sounds naïve in summary, but it had its heroism—and it left a body of work that was not forgotten by the poets who took up his central ideas.

"Language" after Spicer

In a 1985 essay called "Spicer's Language," the poet Ron Silliman describes the continuities between Spicer's work and that of the Language poets of the 1970s and 1980s. First he describes his own debt to Spicer:

> With the exception of the poetry of Barrett Watten, I have quoted, borrowed, appropriated, expropriated, done takes on, paraphrased, parodied or otherwise stolen more sentences, lines, bits or tones from the work of Jack Spicer, often uncritically, than from any other source. (167)

Silliman argues that "overdetermination is the essential Spicerian effect." By "overdetermination" he means the "failure (or refusal) of an idea or image to add up (or reduce down) to a single entity" (169). Elsewhere in the same essay Silliman describes Spicer admiringly as "flooding the text with a surfeit of incommensurable meanings" (185). This last phrase is particularly illuminating as a self-description of Language writing practice, not least the workings of the "new sentence," in which, as he puts it elsewhere, "sentence structure is altered for torque, or increased polysemy/ambiguity" (*The New Sentence,* 91).

But Silliman is restless with what he sees as the drive to "enclosure" in Spicer's writing, even as he admires it. The serial poem, in particular, the poem-as-book, presents this problem of enclosure: "The concerns of *Language* are so thoroughly intertwined from beginning to end that the resulting air of closure borders on the claustrophobic" (169). His key example is the first poem in *Language:*

> This ocean, humiliating in its disguises
> Tougher than anything.
> No one listens to poetry. The ocean
> Does not mean to be listened to. A drop
> Or crash of water. It means
> Nothing.
> It
> Is bread and butter

Pepper and salt. The death
That young men hope for. Aimlessly
It pounds the shore. White and aimless signals. No
One listens to poetry.

For Silliman, the sentence "No one listens to poetry" in line three startles us because it "comes from [an] entirely different [discourse] than the first two lines" (175). So the beginning of the poem is open in a sense, built around unexpected leaps, irreducible to "a single entity." But by the end of the poem, Silliman argues, the word "white," as the only color word in the poem, is clearly deployed "to remind the reader that the poem is an enclosure"—because it comes from a different language than the other words in the poem.

I am not quite persuaded by this interpretation. "No one listens to poetry" makes perfect sense if one assumes that the poet is humiliated by the ocean's ability to outpace even the most comprehensive or apt poetic description; and the poem's sense of "enclosure" seems more emphatically instanced by the final repetition of the sentence, "No / One listens to poetry" than by the arrival of the word "white." But on a more general level, I think Silliman does a splendid job of highlighting the contradictory tendencies at work in Spicer's writing, which I have argued involve both the surprise of invention and the aim of counterenclosure—or, put in more sociable terms, both the induction of new materials into the world through the medium of conversation, gossip, and quarreling, and the sequestration of a subculture that the poet feels must be hidden and scattered inside an enclosing medium in order to survive. Drawing in and keeping out: as Silliman puts it, "If language is conceived of as a medium . . . it is a medium in the sense of a membrane, as capable of blocking the real as it is of letting it in" (181).

What's ironic about his perspicacious reading of the contradictory openness and closedness of Spicer's writing is that Silliman ignores the social context that impelled the contradiction, even as he relies on Spicer to launch an account of the overtly politicized understandings of part-whole relationships so important to the Language writers' sense of poetic value. He misses, in particular, how Spicer's simultaneous disjunctiveness and will to enclosure are shaped by worry about what Boone calls "always-seeming-to-be-impending disaster"—are shaped by worry over the crowding out or paving over of locality by a stream of undifferentiated commodities, or by impending violence, or both.

My sense is that Silliman backs away from more fully contextualizing Spicer because examining the social milieu from which Spicer's poems emerged would only intensify Silliman's sense of the "claustrophobic" aspect of the poetry, its enclosure. Along with other Language writers, Silliman seems to prefer the model of extension and expansion over a model of counterenclosure as a formal means to meet the encroachments of mass culture and its attendant forms of political control.[10]

Shifts of scale, in particular, become an important way for the Language poets to describe their works' relation to political crisis. In a roundtable discussion recorded in Barrett Watten's 1985 book *Total Syntax,* Watten describes Silliman's own writing this way:

> You're never quite sure what the scale of your activity is going to be. The continuity has to be internally produced. There's no way up, or around, or out: the scale could be very great or very little—one doesn't know. Are we in a dire situation or do we have a relatively comfortable life? (23)

Watten is especially articulate about this link between being unable to assess the scalar properties of a writing project and the problem of political "situation" in the privileged first world, where the reverberations of crisis are almost never felt directly. Compare his description of Silliman's long poem to this description of the oil shock of 1973 in terms of a disjunction of scale, or a disjunction between event and medium:

> In 1973 there was the phenomenon of the gas line; here there was a nonfunctional relation between the experience perceived and the belief in doom. We all expect raw materials to run out but no one knows exactly when. And when evidence of the fact actually does occur, the experience itself does not seem like the preexisting dread . . . As opposed to direct perception of the cataclysmic event, we have doom on the far side of the media undermining our brains . . . The necessity for technique is absolute in the face of this fact. (15)

The passage argues that "the media" drown out real analysis of the oil crisis, and implies a temptation to reduce global politics to the inconvenience of waiting in long lines to fill the tanks of our cars. He insists on "the necessity for technique," I think, because for Watten "technique" names a history of anti-aesthetic artistic practice, of practice that aims, not for the autonomy of the artwork, but for its incorporation of alien material—or, better, for an art in which nothing is alien because it is willing to incorporate so much that it becomes uncertain about what is part and what is whole, what is vulnerably open and what autonomous. This is what Watten means by "total syntax"—an art that "continuously argues this edge between self-sufficiency and connection, an art in which "the various linguistic levels—word, line, phrase, sentence, paragraph—each are structural metonyms for 'language' and, ultimately, for 'the writer in time'" (104). It is also what Peter Gizzi, citing Manny Farber in his excellent introduction to the new collected Spicer, calls " 'termite art,' an art that eats its own borders."[11]

Spicer's poems, though, "eat their own borders" through ringing changes on finite elements, or on startling the reader by way of the induction of a specific new element into the poem, so as to heighten the awareness of what's stashed away between its parts. With Language writing, the termite impulse, the impulse toward a "total syntax," is organized around the possibilities of sheer expansiveness. This registers as written mass, in the sheer productivity of so many of the writers of the Language movement, and as the formal gaming with scale that Watten describes in reading Silliman's work. But the termite impulse can also appear, we will see, as a more traditional thematic investigation into the matter of what scale actually is, and even in a thematics of literacy, which poses the question of how the poem fits into the body or the matter of language as a whole.

So the Language poets frequently think of poetry as problem of the vicissitudes of a political and linguistic totality. Where the relation of poetic language to language as a whole was a matter of protectiveness in Spicer, though, the Language writers want their writing to extend outward to meet the language of the spectacle, to match its emulsification of experience with a capaciousness that still makes room for live thought, for surprise, possibly even for politics. Both Spicer and the Language poets want to make use of disorienting juxtaposition to jolt the reader awake, to make her puzzle over part-whole relations—but where Spicer seemed eager to use these strategies to protect a poetic and queer subculture in danger of being marginalized or erased by the rising tides of the Cold War and mass culture, the Language writers turn more often to rhetoric drawn from social movements to stage their own games of vantage shifting.

Consider this untitled poem of Lyn Hejinian's from her 1986 book *The Cell*. The book's multivalent title makes room for the kind of poetry-as-membrane language that Silliman used to describe Spicer's combination of invention and enclosure, but Hejinian makes a feminist use of these dynamics:

In the dark sky there
  are constellations, all of them
  erotic and they break open
  the streets
The streets exceed the house
On occasion the body exceeds
  the self
Every day someone replaces someone and
  someone's mother is sad so
  as to exceed
The bed is a popular
  enclosure from which to depart
Outside the stars are stunning
  —touching
It is a question of
  scale
It is erotic when parts
  exceed their scale

(*The Cell*, 33)

The poem moves wonderfully to embody a figure, the constellation, that from Schleiermacher to Kant to Benjamin has served the ends of helping us imagine forms of part-whole relation that are contingent and open-ended, really part-part relations that imply a whole in progress, yet to be recognized. Here the constellations "eat their context" by how they "break open / the streets," make the streets seem small, or demand that the streets incorporate into our concept of them some sense that they are not complete, that they exist under the stars. The streets obligingly mime this action by repeating it with regard to "the house," which they "break open" by impelling it to open outward onto a context. Hejinian specifies what's erotic about this scalar dynamic of breaking open with her next sentence, "On occasion the body exceeds / the self," fully countercogitating the self by making it most exciting when embodied. This is not a simple valorization of the body over the mind, though, not only because the poem is dealing so thoroughly in concepts of things, but because becoming embodied is quotidian, even when to become one's body is to die: "Every day someone replaces someone and / someone's mother is sad"—as if for every death there were a birth, both of them, "on occasion," framed in horizontally:

"The bed is a popular / enclosure from which to depart." This line stages Hejinian's characteristic comedy—acting here as if where to die and where to be born were matters of "popularity," while embedding the pun on "people" to literalize the joke, to make it simply true as well as funny. But that line also offers an account of the dynamics of enclosure, which the poem reads as innocent inasmuch as enclosure offers launchpads, inasmuch as it is a moment in a dynamic that includes "departure." This is a deliberate counteruse of "enclosure" from its sense of property and privacy, I think, confirmed in its stubbornly comic valence by the final assertion, "It is erotic when parts / exceed their scale." Watten, reading the scalar gaming of a Silliman poem, sees the poem unsettling us so as to keep us in mind of our inability to know the difference between a "dire situation" and a "comfortable life"; Hejinian implies that scalar shifting is not beyond us, that knowing the difference between the stars just being "stunning" and their being "touching," or maybe even literally "touching," is "a question of scale." Attention to the erotic aspect of the formation of concepts makes possible this understanding of scale-shifting as something people are capable of, not just baffled by, much as the social energy of 1980s feminism, with its critiques of the disembodied Cartesian subject as an implicitly masculine model for abstraction, gives a political edge to Hejinian's scalar comedy.

Elsewhere this erotics of scale is called into the service of mediating political and linguistic problems central to the Language-focused writing of the 1980s. Are words things? Are things texts? Michael Palmer pairs these questions with an additional inquiry, which is whether the activity of capital, capturing things to make them commodities, is modeled on how we traverse the word-thing gap, or whether it seizes on our daily acquiescence to the gap being untraversable, and puts that tendency to acquiescence to its own use. Here is a passage from Palmer's poem "The Flower of Capital":

> Capital is a fever at play and in the world (silent *l*) each
> thing is real or must pretend to be. Her tongue swells
> until it fills my mouth. I have lived here for a day or
> part of a day, eyes closed, arms hanging casually at my
> sides. Can such a book be read by you or me?[12]
>
> (*Codes Appearing*, 32–33)

Only a suppression—"silent *l*"—marks the difference between word and world here, and for Palmer it also marks the way in which "each thing" is either real "or must pretend to be," must act as though it is an item for exchange. But this pretence is not only obligation—it is, as in Hejinian, an erotic capacity: "Her tongue swells until it fills my mouth." The sentence blurs illness and eros, fever and sex, as a way of getting at how "capital," though it demands pretense of every thing, enacts that demand by tapping into capabilities—for rising to the occasion, for allure—that could be put to other uses. You could say the fever of capital mimes the fever of eros in order to capture it, to lure it in and redeploy it. Not that this dynamic of capture and mimicry is easily tracked: right by the side of the fevered woman, the poet, unswollen and unpretending, has managed to "live" somewhere with his "Arms hanging casually at [his sides]." How, he asks, can these two things inhabit the same space, these different modes or phases of excitement and inducement, serenity and fever?

"The Flower of Capital" has an epigraph from Spicer: "Not as a gesture of contempt for the scattered nature of reality." So the form of Palmer's paragraph, with its abrupt juxtapositions, follows Spicer explicitly in "scattering" poetic meaning and poetic value across the text, placing its riches in the movement between parts, which yields an argument about capital as the making-swollen of parts, as the capture of that erotic process in the name of the demand that the parts be "real," that they play along with the fever.

Palmer is less interested in construing this movement among poetic units—image, sentence, paragraph—as "magic," in the way Spicer would have, than as a troubled literacy: "Can such a book be read by you or me?" This is in keeping with how both Palmer and the poets more explicitly affiliated with the project of Language writing modulate Spicer's alignment of poetry to linguistics. For Spicer, especially in a book like *Language,* an analogy to linguistic processes like transformation allowed him to sharpen his sense of poetry as the working-over of linguistic interstices:

> Being a [poet] a disyllable in a world of monosyllables. Awakened by the distance between the [o] and the [e]
>
> (243)

For Palmer and the Language poets, though, the "scattered nature of reality" made available by surprising juxtaposition is more interesting for how it lures readers into testing their literacy in scalar shifts. Is Palmer's poem about a sex/fever analogy, or about how capital makes use of a continuity marked by the analogy, or both, and if both, what does that say about our erotic lives as resources for "reading" the text of capital? I think the reading practice poetry like this invites can be back-translated into a kind of question about political agency, which might go something like this: Are the capacities of attention capital makes use of, swelling us up and leaving us deflated, liable to recapture if we resee them on the page, where we might realize how to be more conscious of our own strength, which lies in our susceptibility?

There are many reasons why the Language poets, and their fellow travelers, like Palmer, shift the terms of their analogies to linguistics from a Spicerian investigation of language as magic to a newer investigation of scale-shifting and juxtaposition as tests of literacy. One has to do with a sense that capital itself had both extended its reach and intensified its encroachments into psychic existence, that capital itself had both grown both "bigger" and better able to reach into the crawl spaces of individual citizen-consumers' psyches. Another reason is that linguistics itself changed in the time between Spicer and the Language generation: between the two groups of poets lies the Chomskian revolution, which was beginning to take hold near the time of Spicer's death, but by the 1970s and 1980s had utterly changed the field of linguistics, not least by establishing an analytically influential distinction between what speakers of languages actually said and what they were capable of saying, according to deep rules for language acquisition. Chomsky called this capability linguistic "competence," by which he meant the competence to absorb the rules of a language, any language. The Language writers, picking up on this idea, translated "competence" into something more like "literacy," which has a stronger connotation of skill and participation than the innate capacity suggested by Chomsky's phrase. The Language writers also picked up on the broadest name for Chomsky's theory, "generative linguistics," so called because it foregrounds the innate capacity to generate sentences. Again, though, they reinflected "generative" to mean something more like "productive," leaning on the analogy to linguistics as a way of thinking about poetic form in terms of scale, that is, in terms of part-whole relations among linguistic units, while reinterpreting the universalism of "competence" and "generative" to mean something more literary.[13] So a writer like Hejinian, for instance, in an important 1983 essay called "The Rejection of Closure," could embed the word "generative" in an argument more about literacy and poetic form than about the linguistic observation about innate capacity to recognize structure:

> We can say that a "closed text" is one in which all the elements of the work are directed toward a single reading of it. Each element confirms that reading and delivers the text from any lurking ambiguity. In the "open text," meanwhile, all the elements of the work are maximally excited . . .
>
> The "open text," by definition, is open to the world and particularly to the reader. It invites participation, rejects the authority of the writer over the reader and thus, by analogy, the authority implicit in other (social, economic, cultural) hierarchies. It speaks for writing that is generative rather than directive. (*Language of Inquiry,* 42–43)

In this passage, "generativity" is ascribed to texts, then to the kinds of relations between writer and reader that the text encourages or models. In 1983 the passage would have resonated, not only with a feminist critique of how gender hierarchies encode themselves in reading and writing, but with a broad swath of progressive ideas linking literacy and political empowerment that were emerging in the work of North Americans like Henri Giroux and anticolonialist Latin Americans like Paulo Freire.

Hejinian's remarks are interesting for how they mediate between two overlapping arguments in Language writing about the relationship between scale and the experience of form. As I detailed above, writers like Barrett Watten and Ron Silliman foreground the aspect of bafflement and disorientation that comes from "flooding the text with a surfeit of incommensurable meanings," or from not knowing "what the scale of your activity is going to be." Hejinian, in her advocacy of a writing that just keeps going, that "rejects closure," seems akin to the arguments of Watten and Silliman. But her emphasis on participatory, even empowering, relation between writer and reader runs quietly against the language of disorientation and bafflement. The two arguments are not opposite: one can easily imagine a pedagogy in which disorientation is used to reorient the reader, to make her more agile and alert. But it is an unstable mixture nonetheless.

Some poets seized on exactly this instability: what if the reading practice of scalar shifting were both disorienting and somehow enabling? Or better—what if the mix between disorientation and empowerment could be discovered only in the production of poetic forms, which could then tell us where we stood—what the ratio was between our bafflement and our alertness. This is to reintroduce suppressed aesthetic matters into language writing, of course: in this model of using the poem's form to read our political capacities back to us, "form" becomes, once more, Adorno's "sun-dial of history," less like "termite art" or sheer linguistic mass and more like a sensitive gauge of what we can or can't still remain alive to. This freights "literacy" with both aesthetic and political meanings.

Take Michael Palmer's poem "Sun," from his 1988 book of the same name. The poem tries to understand the violence of the war in Vietnam by exploring what it has done to our ability or inability to read and write. Here are the first few lines:

> SUN
>
> Write this. We have burned all their villages
> Write this. We have burned all the villages and the people in them
> Write this. We have adopted their customs and their manner of dress
> Write this. A word may be shaped like a bed, a basket of tears or an X
>
> (*Codes Appearing*, 233)

The instructional scene begins in horror and modulates to curiosity as it ranges from commands that seem to suit the scene of a grammar, or a rhetoric, or a linguistics seminar. One way to measure this movement would be to say we start out being asked to feel the moral weight of the first two "examples," then the grim historical irony of the third, in which the erasure of the villages and their people is written over by their invaders, their replacements, who mime what they have destroyed. The fourth "example," then, implicitly mimics the movement between the first two and the third, so that morphological indifference—"a word may be shaped like a bed, a basket of tears, or an X"—offers a beautiful and upsetting range of concretion to flesh out the meaning of the movement of what came before it.

So we are emphatically in the scene of acquiring literacy, though in a mixed mode: at what scale, and with what concern or indifference to the content of the sample sentences? The poem that develops from this astonishing opening works by way of a mischievous elasticity in the persona of the poet, a Spicerian trickster-teacher—"For a nickel I will appear from this box," he writes—who is now also a party to colonial violence. This elasticity of persona is itself enabled by what we could call a scale-jumping in which our attention is directed from historical violence, to the shapes of words, to the acquisition of language, and finally (we will see) to a kind of abécédaire. This is the brilliance of the poem: its pathos and its force derive from how this mock pedagogy is never entirely unhitched from imagining a real scene of writing, where the poet and his students or his readers must confront the variable actuality of the examples presented to them.

What is the relation of the acquiring of literacy to the assuming of historical responsibility? The poem's answer to this question seems to be that both require similar skills, and have a similar allure: knowing how to experience part-whole relations in a mobile and reflexive way.

Midway through the poem Palmer shifts from a Spicerian gaming of invention and disposition—of repeating pieces of language in variable order—to something different, something on another scale: a reflection on the condition of creation and mimesis in the face of violence. Here is the transition:

> Say this. I was born on an island among the dead. I learned
> language on this island but did not speak on this island. I am
> writing to you from this island. I am writing to the dancers from
> this island. The writers do not dance on this island
> Say this. There is a sentence in my mouth, there is a chariot in my
>   mouth. There is a ladder. There is a lamp whose light fills empty space
>   and a space which swallows light
>
> (234)

Except for the instruction, "Say this," the first of the two strophes is right out of Spicer, with its repetition of "this island" alongside the shifting arrangement of "dancers" and "writers" "writing." Its theme of numbness and joylessness shifts in the next strophe to a more symbolist mode—what does it mean to say one has a "chariot" in one's mouth?

I think Palmer asks us to decide what that "chariot" might mean by reading it out of what comes before and after it. The shocking first line is still with us—"Write this. We have burned all their villages"—and it colors what comes after. It becomes easier, for instance, to read the poet as saying that the "sentence" and the "chariot" are linked in the hegemon's mouth, the mouth of the speaker who burns villages. I don't think it's fanciful, given the reading practice the poem encourages, to read the "ladder" as the fateful link between the sentence and the chariot, whether as the fatal implication of the speaker with violence, or as the guilty wish that writing were inventive only, were innocent. Palmer does not presume to decide, but keeps returning to tropes of extinguishment: "There is a lamp whose light fills empty space and a space which swallows light." Writing is torn here not between a mirror and a lamp, description and invention, but between the lamp and its destruction. The fate of the "sentence" is not light.

The poem has terror in it, partly because of how it modulates the pedagogical practice Boone ascribes to Spicer—"You better be careful . . . you might miss the point if you [aren't]"—into a darker key, where even the trickster-teacher is unsure of the line between instruction in invention ("write this") and sheer indoctrination. I say this because the poem deliberately mimics, not only the classroom, but the practice of ideology, ideology in the sense Althusser means when he refers to Pascal's *Pensées:* "Kneel down, move your lips in prayer, and you will believe" ("Ideology and Ideological State Apparatus," 169).[14]

You might say that the disaster Boone thinks Spicer wanted to warn his initiates to be alert to, which had already arrived in the form of Hiroshima, the murder of the European Jews, or the assassination of John F. Kennedy, has rearrived, this time with the unavoidable implication of American observers in the violence of the event. So Spicer's sleights of hand, his plays of invention, are modulated in Palmer to include the scale shifting that seems necessary to meet a totality ever more extensive and intensive, and this modulation is not so much in the service of countering ideology, or the spectacle, as in miming it, trying to keep pace with it, to see which resources of language it has and has not captured.

But this is a difficult thing to measure, and the attempt takes the poem to a place of unknowing: the reading practice it encourages does not, finally, look like a recipe for readerly empowerment. "Sun" concludes with a darkly comic abécédaire where the objectivity of "writing" lies outside the classroom scene of the poet's inventions:

> Let me say this. Neak Luong is a blur. It is Tuesday in the hardwood
>   forest. I am a visitor here, with a notebook
> The notebook lists My New Words and Flag above White. It
> claims to have no inside
>   only characters like A-against-Herself, B,
> C, L and N, Sam, Hans Magnus, T. Sphere, all speaking in the
> dark with their hands
>   G for Gramsci or Goebbels, blue hills, cities,
> cities with hills, modern and at the edge of time
>   F for
> alphabet, Z for A, an H in an arbor, shadow, silent wreckage, W or M
>   among stars
> What last. Lapwing. Tesseract. X perhaps for X. The villages are

> known as These Letters—humid, sunless. The writing occurs on
> their walls
>
> (235)

The teacher is now a tourist, a student, a witness—"Let me say this"—hovering around an illegally bombed Cambodia where the place makes his sense of time irrelevant, aesthetic heroes are mute, and the granular low to which his language is reduced tells him nothing about the moral valence of the medium, which seems to have none ("G for Gramsci or Goebbels"). He games as best he can, brilliantly, deliberately misreading "F" as its sound ("F for alphabet"), seeing "Z" as the ouribouros-end of a circular alphabet, making a harbor from an "arbor," hearing the silence in the "H" as a preview and a miming of the silence of the "W" in "wreckage," then revaluing the "W" and an "M" into gendered persons, Woman and Man, themselves visually reversible as constellations in the night sky.

But none of it flies. "Lapwing" and "Tesseract" jump scale dizzyingly, from bird to hypergeometric cube, but "the villages" that return at the end of the poem are unmoved: "humid, sunless." They are their own book, possibly a Vietnamese translation of the book of Daniel, where "writing" in the script of the dominated first appears on imperial walls to foretell an empire's fall.[15]

It's as though Palmer's opening lines, so emphatic in their implication of the poet and his readers in violence, cannot make the turn to the medium character of language meet the moral challenge of the poem's beginning. The dark virtuosity of the final strophes recalls Spicer's attempts to mine poetic gold out of the interstices of the grapheme, the morpheme, the phoneme. But where Spicer still believed in a kind of card-trick magic by which rhetorical invention could colonize even the building blocks of language and make them sing, Palmer clearly feels that the poet's skill in producing distraction has come frighteningly close to the modes of distraction that enable collective consent for colonial violence. In light of this dilemma, the poem's turn to prophecy feels inevitable, as if it were the only pressure valve left to release the burden of implication the wildly inventive poet still carries. It is this prophetic turn that distinguishes Palmer both from Spicer and from the Language poets with whom he is sometimes affiliated. But it is not unequivocal: as in Milton's "Hymn on the Morning of Christ's Nativity," the "Oracles are dumm." For Milton, the silence of the oracles was a triumphant sign of the end of pagan prophecy and the dawn of a salvation unheralded by the old civilization it would displace; for Palmer, whose "Sun" is filled with figures of muteness and dumbness, the silence of the "humid, sunless" "letters" of the closing prophecy implies another historical transition, but from what to what? From the resistant energies of the 1960s, whose moral force the poem relies upon, to the defeats of the 1980s, when it was written? Or some other, harder-to-name transition?

This is where the generation of poets who came after the turn to "language" are left: a sense that the playful distractions language makes possible are breathlessly close to the ideology of the spectacle, and—even worse—a worry that the prophetic mode has itself become "dumb," that one cannot handle it without some kind of distance, a distance that might negate the turn to prophecy in the first place. In the next and final chapter I offer an outline of the poetry being written under these contradictory conditions.

— 4 —
Bubble and Crash: Poetry in Late-Late Capitalism

I want to conclude with a look at recent poetry written under conditions that might best be understood by a look backward from 2009, when I was finishing up this book. In 2003 I wrote an essay, the germ of this chapter, called "Camp Messianism, or, The Hopes of Poetry in Late-Late Capital." In that piece I sketched a structure of poetic feeling by which, it seemed to me, left-leaning poets working in the generation after the emergence of Language writing were trying to understand how to name the experience of an extreme, felt "lateness" in capitalism. I found that, in various ways, those writers mingled the rhetorics of camp and of left-wing messianism in order to name a present that seemed, as I say, both very "late" but also undescribable by way of figures of lateness. What emerged from these blended rhetorics, I felt, was something like a lightly camp attitude *toward* messianism—a sense that the language of revolutionary end-times could now only be appropriated like the other kinds of superseded waste-products to which camp practices and languages have fastened themselves—with a kind of fond defiance of its obsolescence, or with what I called, at the time, "polemical affection."

Then came the economic crisis of 2008, and abruptly "capitalism" was pronounceable for the first time in decades as the name, not of an inevitability, but of a contingent economic form: the October 18, 2008, edition of *The Economist,* for instance, bemoaned "Capitalism at Bay," while the February 7, 2009, edition of *Newsweek* featured a cover article called "We Are All Socialists Now." At the same time, however, mass-circulation writing about the crisis never actually raised the question of what else besides capitalism we might want to imagine constructing. Even *Harper's,* certainly on the left end of wide-circulation news magazines in the United

States, took a reformist position on the crisis, publishing a series of essays on "How to Save Capitalism" (November 2008).

Of course it would be unrealistic to expect American economic journalism to envision a social form other than capitalism; its imaginative bar has always been very low. What's more noteworthy is the rhetorical whiplash, and the logical confusion, that emerges from the writing that tries to address how average citizens should react to the crisis. I would like to spend a moment with some of this writing—I've chosen from among many examples on offer in 2008–2009—because I think its incoherence is cousin to the strange, unstable rhetoric produced by the left-leaning poets we'll be looking at in this chapter. If the poets of this period struggle with how to imagine the unimaginable—an end to capitalism without a conceivable revolution—mass-circulation writing about the crisis struggles with a related impossibility, which is how to imagine changing capitalism from within, when the only option seems to be to continue doing exactly what caused the crisis in the first place. I think a brief look at this nonpoetic writing will help us be able to read the poetry, not only as part of a history of literary writing on the left, or part of a history of avant-garde experiment, but also as part of a broad cultural effort to think and live inside the contradictions of capital.

Take, for instance, the *Newsweek* piece, "We Are All Socialists Now." The title is an attempt to sensationalize Richard Nixon's comment, at the beginning of the economic slump of the 1970s, that "we are all Keynesians now." And indeed, *Newsweek* turns out to mean nothing more, in its use of the word "socialism," than Keynesianism—that is, government management of the economy designed to modulate the worst of capitalism's tendencies to crisis, or, in the language of the day, "more government." It is surely a measure of the success of the post-1980 right wing that *Newsweek* can equate Keynesian economics with socialism; leaving that aside, though, let's look at a key paragraph from the article:

> Now comes the reckoning. The answer may indeed be more government. In the short run, since neither consumers nor business is likely to do it, the government will have to stimulate the economy. And in the long run, an aging population and global warming and higher energy costs will demand more government taxing and spending. The catch is that more government intrusion in the economy will almost surely limit growth (as it has in Europe, where a big welfare state has caused chronic high unemployment).

> Growth has always been America's birthright and saving grace. (Meacham and Thomas)

Again, leaving aside the question of the validity of the claim about welfare states and unemployment, look at the theological language of the passage. Reckoning, birthright, grace: the dents in the system of finance trigger a panic in which all that can be grasped is a religious paradox—the paradox that "government" both "stimulates" the "economy" and "limits" something called "growth," mingling grace and punishment, profligacy and austerity. This paradox, created by an implicit definition of "growth" in which growth counts only if it's infinite and perpetual—that is, if it's capitalist—this paradox cannot be tamed by the writers of the piece except by the unstably naturalizing figure of aging and its unwanted effects. As they put it, "As boomers age and spending grows, we will become even more French."

So the large-scale contradiction between infinite growth and the preservation of welfare is felt by economic journalists as an irresolvable paradox that can be stomached only by way of a naturalizing figure for unnaturalness: aging as—horror!—becoming French. But the contradiction does not only register on a large scale. One of the more puzzling messages sent by economists to the average citizen during the crash was that they could help pull the country out of its slump by spending more, but only if they also saved more. Here too, economic journalists were quick to note the contradiction, and to sequester it from political implications by rewriting it as a paradox, then rewriting the paradox through figures of resignation. In a 2009 article on Americans' relationship to shopping malls, for instance, David Segal of the *New York Times* wrote:

> Here, ladies and gentlemen, is the crux of the problem: We are reliably informed that whatever part of the economic crisis can't be pinned on Wall Street—or on mortgage-related financial insanity—can be pinned on consumers who overspent. But personal consumption amounts to some 70 percent of the American economy. So if we don't spend, we don't recover. Fiscal health isn't possible until money is again sloshing into cash registers, including those at this mall and every other retailer.
>
> In other words, shopping was part of the problem and now it's part of the cure. And once we're cured, economists report, we really need to learn how to save, which suggests that we will need to quit shopping again.

> So the mall we married has become the toxic spouse we can't quit, though we really must quit, but just not any time soon. The mall, for its part, is wounded by our ambivalence and feels financially adrift.
>
> Like any other troubled marriage, this one needs counseling. And pronto, because even a trial separation at a moment as precarious as this could get really ugly. ("Our Love Affair with Malls")

The jaunty irony of the piece ("We are reliably informed" . . . "And pronto") cannot mask that what is on offer is a recipe for taking our lumps. Consumers are blamed for doing what the postwar economic system has continuously solicited them to do—"overspend"—and their punishment is to be stuck with a "toxic spouse" whose toxicity, it is never quite acknowledged, amounts to abuse. Segal's one droll image of financial health—"money . . . sloshing into cash registers"—speaks plainly enough to the meagerness of what the "marriage counseling" will eventually yield.

Rhetoric like this forms part of what the sociologist Randy Martin has called "the financialization of daily life"—a process by which business journalism and mass-market financial advising collude with the aims of postwar economic planning to produce, not only the citizen as consumer, but the consumer as a subject who uses the language of business of organize her psychic life. Martin is especially persuasive when he discusses the role that an ideology of "risk" has played in this process, which he roughly dates from the 1970s. Among the key elements in this process of orienting subjects around the experience of risk, Martin argues, have been historical developments in the labor market and in the financial sector. He suggests that the restructuring of pension plans from defined-benefit to defined-contribution models, for instance, effectively hitched millions of future retirees more closely than ever to the ups and downs of the marketplace; and that the financial sector's race to securitize debt (that is, bundle and disperse it) and sell it has produced a "socialization of risk"—a suggestion more than borne out by the dynamics of the 2008–2009 financial crisis. He is breathtakingly clear on this last point:

> Securitization is the new millennium's version of eighteenth-century Enclosure Acts. Whereas peasants had to be physically removed from common lands to dispossess them of property . . . Possession has been rendered liquid so that it can be revalued daily. The active pulse of money in motion is the medium through which occasions arise to move physically from place to place as a job or a home can no longer bear the

> demand for increased value placed upon it. (*Financialization of Daily Life*, 141–142)

The people who have endured this mass dispossession, whether it takes the form of the destruction of retirement income or the loss of homes and jobs, have no strong public language to give shape to the experience; what they have, instead, is the ironic resignation of journalism after the crash, which has made it seem inevitable; and, behind that rhetoric, a steady diet of business-press cheerleading that has intensified since the 1970s.

Compare the language, for instance, of two financial-advice best-sellers, Bernard Malkiel's 1973 *A Random Walk down Wall Street*, and Nassim Nicholas Taleb's *The Black Swan: The Impact of the Highly Improbable*, from 2007. Martin identifies Malkiel as an early prophet of the socialization of risk based on passages like this, where he urges members of the emerging small-investor class to expose themselves to the market's chances:

> Common sense attests that some people can and do beat the market. It's not all chance. Many academics agree; but the method of beating the market, they say, is not to exercise superior clairvoyance but to assume greater risk. Risk, and risk alone, determines the degree to which returns will be above or below average. (Martin 120)

This passage was written at the beginning of the era of financialization, when the idea of making workers become stakeholders in their own retirement—either by accepting pensions hitched to the stock market, or by becoming small players on it—seemed like a cure to the economic stagnation of the early 1970s. Thirty-five years later, after the destruction of shareholders' retirement security in the collapse of Long Term Capital Management (1998) and Enron (2001), the purveyors of this rhetoric have had to ramp up the language of risk exponentially in order to maintain its persuasiveness—not least by acknowledging the link between the movement of capital and the creation of disaster.

Taleb's *Black Swan* is a kind of apotheosis of risk encouragement. Taleb is both a former day trader and an outspoken critic of the Wall Street risk-modeling practices of the 1990s and the early years of the twenty-first century that reduced complex and widely different measures to single daily measures—but he is not a critic of risk orientation per se, just a critic of the idea that risk can be predicted. As Joe Nocera of the *New York Times* put it, in a profile of Taleb,

> [he argues that] the greatest risks are never the ones you can see and measure, but the ones you can't see and therefore can never measure. The ones that seem so far outside the boundary of normal probability that you can't imagine they could happen in your lifetime—even though, of course, they do happen, more often than you care to realize. Devastating hurricanes happen. Earthquakes happen. And once in a great while, huge financial catastrophes happen. Catastrophes that risk models somehow always manage to miss. ("Risk Mismanagement")

These unforeseeable catastrophes are what Taleb calls "black swans"—and despite his self-positioning as a philosopher of history, they form the basis of a kind of second-order investment advice—in which risk needs to be not only embraced, as in Malkiel's book, but made into a universal causal principle of the unforeseeable. Here is a passage from the prologue to Taleb's book:

> Just imagine how little your understanding of the world on the eve of the events of 1914 would have helped you guess what was to happen next . . . How about the rise of Hitler and the subsequent war? How about the precipitous demise of the Soviet bloc? How about the rise of Islamic fundamentalism? How about the spread of the Internet? How about the market crash of 1987 . . . ? (*The Black Swan,* xviii)

He concludes: "It is easy to see that life is the cumulative effect of a handful of significant shocks" (xix). Taleb offers, then, not so much offer practical investment advice as a theodicy of volatility, and a kind of apotheosis of the genre of financial advice writing—which has blown up into a manic outlook ("How about . . . how about . . .") that sees disaster everywhere, and that, instead of trying to understand its causes, urges a kind of pretraumatic paranoia about its perpetually imminent arrival.

In advising this comportment Taleb is perhaps the perfect prophet of what Naomi Klein has called "disaster capitalism"—her phrase for a stage of capitalist history in which the demands of liquidity achieve a scale and intensity that puts states, economies, and ecosystems in danger; indeed, Klein argues, at this stage of capital, liquidity *seeks out* disaster, because disaster is the only instrument capable of producing truly "free" conditions for capital expansion. Klein fleshes out this startling claim with a genealogy of free-market revolts against postwar Keynesianism that center on the work of Milton Friedman, whose influence in turning the capitalist world away from that Keynesianism, and toward a Reagan-Thatcher model of free-market economics, is deep. She cites Friedman's introduction to his 1962 *Capitalism and Freedom,* where he writes, "Only a crisis—actual or perceived—produces real change" (Klein 140). She also notes the remarks of a student of Friedman's mentor, the Austrian economist Friedrich Hayek, who describes Hayek's hatred of any state intervention in the economy at all: "It's as if there is a very pretty but highly complex picture out there, which is perfectly harmonious within itself, you see, and if there's a speck where it isn't supposed to be, well, that's just awful . . . it is a flaw that mars the beauty" (53). Elsewhere Klein glosses the link between Hayek's purist aesthetics of the market and Friedman's crisis theory:

> This desire for godlike powers of total creation is precisely why free-market ideologues are so drawn to crises and disasters. Nonapocalyptic reality is simply not hospitable to their ambitions. For thirty-five years, what has animated Friedman's counterrevolution is an attraction to a kind of freedom and possibility available only in times of cataclysmic change. (20–21)

One of the achievements of Klein's book is that she makes it possible to describe those last thirty-five years as a coherent history of global capitalism, in which political crises, natural disasters, and economic upheavals alike are swept up in the rage for unimpeded value expansion, from the restructuring of Chile's economy after the assassination of Salvador Allende in 1973, to the mass privatization of the public resources of the countries of the former Soviet bloc in the early 1990s, to the profiteering after the 2004 Indian Ocean earthquake and tsunami, and the privatization of social services in New Orleans after Hurricane Katrina in 2005.

If Klein makes it possible to begin to narrate the history of the most recent phase of global capitalism through a series of political, environmental, and financial disasters, the best recent poetry allows us to see something like that history's obverse—the story of how selves are solicited to participate in this phase of the life of capital, and of how they struggle to respond to the tones of that solicitation, which range, of course, from murmur to threat.

Sadness and Securitization: Claudia Rankine

Take this passage from Claudia Rankine's 2004 *Don't Let Me Be Lonely,* which uses a mixture of lists, images, and poetic prose to look back on the dot-com boom of the 1990s from midway through the Bush administration:

> To roll over or not roll over that IRA? To have a new iMac or not to have it? To eTrade or not to eTrade? Again and again these were Kodak moments, full of individuation; we were all on our way to our personal best. America was seemingly a meritocracy. I, I, I am Tiger Woods. It was the nineties. Now it is the twenty-first century and you are either with us or you are against us. Where is your flag? (91)

Rankine reworks Hamlet's soliloquy, so often positioned as the birth of modern selfhood, from after the end of posthistory, when the existentially thin questions of "individuation" on offer in the 1990s congeal into a different kind of question, the glowering post-9/11 interrogation, "Where is your flag?" for which there is only one correct answer. This whiplash return-of-history also collapses the postracial "meritocracy" by which Rankine could ironically echo herself into position, back then: "I, I, I am Tiger Woods." The shareholder culture of the 1990s, which would prefigure the cut-rate homeowner culture of the next boom, conceived of every citizen as a potential winner on the stock market—indeed, imagined a world of only winners, which fantasy Rankine cleverly glosses in her campy turn to sports language ("personal best" is also the title of a 1982 film about lesbian runners) and in her crowding Tiger Woods with multiple "I's."

Woods is, of course, crowded with "I's" in the American imaginary, because he is a figure for complexly mixed racial identity; and Rankine's converting the reconciliatory valences of Wood's race into a metaphor for crowding, for unrealistic expectations, is one way she marks historical time in *Don't Let Me Be Lonely.* Elsewhere she turns to another mixed-race figure of posthistory, Keanu Reeves's character Neo from *The Matrix,* to mark the transition from the bubble to its aftermath once more:

> When she comes toward me I stiffen. But it's all right. It's nothing. The pamphlet says in bold letters, **BE LIKE JESUS.** Because I was brought up this way, I walk two blocks before tossing it. Be your own Christ. I'll remember that or I remember that. As if it were a soul memory, I say aloud to Neo, be like Jesus. I am on my way home from seeing *The Matrix Reloaded.* The film's superhero, Neo, can't save anyone; Morpheus will have to have another dream: the one in which salvation narratives are passé; the one in which people live no matter what you dream; the one in which

> people die no matter what you dream; or no matter what, you dream. (121)

Joshua Clover has suggested that the first film in *The Matrix* trilogy (*The Matrix,* 1999) offered a version of "the dreamlife of the boom"—that is, a fantasy of heroic hackers outmaneuvering the megacorporations that both gave them amazing toys to play with and colonized their daily lives, blasting past the eight-hour workday (*The Matrix,* 73). It was also, in its blending of the choreography of Asian martial arts films with the iconography of sixties radicalism and Black Power, and its casting of Reeves as Neo, a fantasy of the postracial future—or, more specifically, a fantasy that attempted to mediate between strong associations of Asianness with technology and futurity, on the one hand, and blackness with the past and violence, on the other.

Rankine leans cannily on these associations to rewrite her encounter with a street evangelist in terms of their decay. If *The Matrix* was the great postracial allegory of the boom, she suggests, then the first of its two sequels is already a symptom of what came after—a crash; a war. Neo's inability to "save anyone" in *The Matrix Reloaded* (2003) is only part of Rankine's reworked allegory; the film was broadly panned for succumbing to action-movie clichés and for taking the slyly messianic tropology of the first film and pumping it up into something that crowded out all the earlier film's nimble plotting and efficient character sketches. The franchise, succumbing to the spectacular logic its prequel seemed to critique, became as disposable as the boldfaced pamphlet the poet tosses aside.

Rankine's suggestion that the idea of the end of history is now a kind of disposable waste ("salvation narratives are passé") turns her thoughts in a different direction, to the burdens of history, especially the burden of racial violence and its repercussions in the emotional lives of those who witness it. Much of *Don't Let Me Be Lonely* struggles with this problem, which we might describe as the struggle to give meaning to broken lives, or meaning to death, in a context where historical hope seems passé, and where its becoming passé is explicitly linked to its having ballooned into an empty spectacle. The simple word Rankine uses for this problem is "sad"—a word that appears throughout the book, and that she links to racial violence, historical hope, and the value of life.

The word comes up, for instance, in a meditation on the death of James Byrd Jr.—a 49-year-old black man who was dragged to his death, tied to a truck, in Jasper, Texas, in 1998. Rankine accuses George W. Bush of not caring about the death because he could not recall the details of the case (it was very high-profile, and he was governor of Texas at the time). Then she writes:

> I forget things too. It makes me sad. Or it makes me the saddest. The sadness is not really about George W. or our American optimism; the sadness lives in the recognition that a life can not matter. Or, as there are billions of lives, my sadness is alive alongside the recognition that billions of lives never mattered. I write this without breaking my heart, without bursting into anything. Perhaps this is the real source of my sadness. Or, perhaps, Emily Dickinson, my love, hope was never a thing with feathers. I don't know, I just find when the news comes on I switch the channel. This new tendency might be indicative of a deepening personality flaw: IMH, The Inability to Maintain Hope, which translates into no innate trust in the supreme laws that govern us. Cornel West says this is what is wrong with black people today—too nihilistic. Too scarred by hope to hope, too experienced to experience, too close to dead is what I think. (23)

Rankine's indictment of Bush almost immediately becomes a query to herself, a forlorn investigation of the "deepening personality flaw" that, like her deflated retirement account, acquires an acronym—"IMH"—and that teeters on the edge of pathologization. But she demurs from Cornel West's diagnosis of black "nihilism" in favor of a contradictory and tendential account of sad blackness and black sadness: "too scarred by hope to hope"—and "too close to dead." This relation to death has a history; it's someplace people are *headed.* And though that history is older by far than the phase of capitalism Rankine inhabits, she insists again and again that part of what keeps it in the register of inarticulate pain is the way it becomes spectacular—part of the news, just what's on TV. Indeed, the epigraph to the book, taken from Aimé Césaire's *Notebook of a Return to My Native Land* (1939), addresses this problem directly:

> And most of all beware, even in thought, of assuming the sterile attitude of the spectator, for life is not a spectacle, a sea of grief is not a proscenium, a man who wails is not a dancing bear.

I'll say more in a bit about the role of television in Rankine's book, and its relation to her idea of what poetry is, and can do. But first I'd like to counterpose the camp or discarded messianism of the earlier passages, and her wariness about the spectacularization of injury, with a scene she describes about three-quarters of the way through the book:

> We have just seen George Wein's documentary, *Louis Armstrong at Newport, 1971.* In the auditorium a room full of strangers listened to Mahalia Jackson sing "Let There Be Peace on Earth" and stood up and gave a standing ovation to a movie screen. Her clarity of vision crosses thirty years to address intimately each one of us. It is as if her voice has always been dormant within each of us, waiting to be awakened, even though "it had to go through its own lack of answers, through terrifying silence, (and) through the thousand darknesses of murderous speech."
>
> Perhaps Mahalia, like Paul Celan, has already lived all our lives for us. Perhaps that is the definition of genius. Hegel says, "Each man hopes and believes he is better than the world which is his, but the man who is better merely expresses the same world better than the others." Mahalia Jackson sings as if it is the last thing she intends to do. And even though the lyrics of the song are, "Let there be peace on earth and let it begin with me," I am hearing, *Let it begin in me.* (97)

While this is by no means a "salvation narrative," it is a counterweight to the falsely posthistorical uses to which the images of Tiger Woods and Reeves's Neo are put. Like those others, the image and the voice of Jackson have their own temporal power, "cross[ing] thirty years" and "awakening" dormant capacities in its latter-day auditors (in this power the image of Jackson is less like *The Matrix*'s Neo than like its Oracle, a renegade program inside the matrix but waveringly independent of it—played as a grandmotherly black woman by the late, alluring Gloria Foster). Her message—and it comes across as that, a *message*—draws from Rankine and the other audience members an ovation that Rankine can't help but note, with an irony now tender, is directed at a ghost—an object, a lost thing, "a movie screen." But this scene, so exactly a mimicry of the work of the spectacle, outmaneuvers it because it remains marked as human, as vulnerable. The image has a minor, out-of-date vehicle, a thirty-year-old documentary; and Jackson's interpretation of the song seems to highlight her own finiteness. She sings, Rankine says, "as if it is the last thing she intends to do."

This performance addresses the problem of the multitudes in a different way than Rankine's earlier, despairing confrontation of "billions" of lives that "can not matter." Not only do the dated image and vulnerable voice ignite something present in the poet, that is, but she seems to have encapsulated countless lives, lived them so as to be able to make awake for later listeners a working of life inside each of them—which is what Rankine tries to grasp and paraphrase by her citations of Paul Celan and Hegel.

Indeed, we could say that the appearance of Jackson in the poem excites citation, and draws attention to the textually networked character of *Don't Let Me Be Lonely.* Throughout the book Rankine draws on what we might think of as her poetry's cousins and antecedents—Hegel, Celan, Milosz, Vallejo, and Césaire, for instance, establishing touchstones for the poet, many of which center on remarks about happiness and suffering. The arc of these citations concludes on the last pages of the book, where Rankine cites Celan once more, quoting his famous 1960 letter to Hans Bender, in which he compares a poem and a handshake (130). If the quote from Hegel establishes the register of the world-historical as a kind of outer limit to the book's meditations, Celan's remark about a poem being like a handshake confirms that for Rankine the history of the world, at least as tracked by poetry, is written in that history's integuments and ligatures—in protective coverings, connective gestures.

One of the functions of this work of citations, I think, is to protect the poet and her work from being drowned out by other media—not least television, which threatens to numb and depress the poet by making all life, because it streams uninterruptedly at her through the screen, equally worthless. But there is no absolute dichotomy in Rankine's book between poetry and television, between life that "can not matter" and the work of genius that connects each life. Instead Rankine slyly acknowledges the allure of TV, as well as a variety of other media films, Internet search engines, and newspaper writing. Rankine makes analogies to these other media throughout *Don't Let Me Be Lonely,* using them to establish a poetic method through which the uncertain value of life can be tested out.

To trace just one of these analogies: the book is printed in a tall, slender format that invites analogy to the experience of newspaper reading, and indeed is set in Imperial, a typeset the publishers note was originally designed in the 1920s at the behest of "American newspaper publishers looking for fonts more suitable for newspaper reading." The book's subtitle calls the volume "An American Lyric," and though the "poems" are largely written in prose paragraphs, with occasional modulations into lineated verse, Rankine maintains a lyric attitude toward her materials in at least two ways. One is by highlighting the movements of her mind, especially her associative leaps and startling juxtapositions. The other, which I've already mentioned, is to develop her practice of citation—which includes not only the work of other poets, and of philosophers, but song lyrics, overheard conversation, the content of news articles. This second practice, while not exclusively "lyric," nonetheless sets in motion a perpetual analogy *between* "lyric" (which is, after all, the book's master term) and the other textual and linguistic forms it records. By halfway through the book, then, it is possible to read even Rankine's vertical reprinting of the roster of the Pharmaceutical Manufacturer's Association of South Africa as a "poem" (115–116). This material, in all its variety, alters the typeface-and-page-size analogy to the newspaper, so that more than lyricized "news," *Don't Let Me Be Lonely* comes to feel like a scrapbook or commonplace book.

This scrapbooking includes photos and logos and drawings alongside her prose paragraphs and lineated verse, not least images of a television, with one version of the image—a TV screen showing only static—serving as a section marker throughout the book. Elsewhere the images shown on these TV screens are unsubtly clipped into the screen's space, looking more like still photos PhotoShopped onto an image of a TV than like photos of what a television is showing, much less like actual screen captures. The artificiality of these images is emphasized by the repetition of the static-screen TV, which seems to highlight the insistent presence of an image-stream both as a toxic or atonal part of the book's lyric surround, but also as an ironic domestication of the image stream, which is made slightly comic by the presence of the televisions themselves, and by the relatively low-tech simulation of their appearance on the page.

The textual environment Rankine assembles thus establishes "lyric" as a master category meant to be intellectually powerful enough to withstand the intrusions of the image stream, even to take energy from it, even to mock it. But because the book also positions itself as a personal and idiosyncratic collection of clippings, it also foregrounds the vulnerability of the scrapbook in the face of the spectacle. There is no final adjudication in this pas de deux between the will to power of the lyric and the humility of the scrapbook, no judgment day—after all, "Salvation narratives are passé." At one key point, Rankine does make recourse to a notion of The Book to flesh out her theme—but that book is not the Bible. It is, rather, the dictionary—which, along with the Bible, plays such an important role in the history of literacy, not least the history of black literacy, where encounters with the word, and learning to read, are crucial to stories of slavery and the escape from slavery. Rankine consults the dictionary to make sense of the value of life, to situate herself in a global context, and to establish the lateral resonance of her key theme—the many meanings of the word "sad." She describes a visit to her grandmother in a nursing home:

> In third-world countries I have felt overwhelmingly American, calcium-rich, and white. Here, I feel young, lucky, and sad. Sad is one of those words that has given its life up for our country, it's been a martyr for the American dream, it's been neutralized, co-opted by our culture to suggest a tinge of discomfort that lasts the time it takes to change a channel. But sadness is real because once it meant something real. It meant dignified, grave; it meant trustworthy; it meant exceptionally bad, deplorable, shameful; it meant massive, weighty, forming a compact body; it meant falling heavily; and it meant of a color: dark. It meant dark in color, to darken. It meant me. I felt sad. (108)

So imagining the dictionary as the guarantor of feeling has a similar function as imagining the book of poems as a scrapbook: it allows the poet to move among citations, to gird her sense of self in a situation that threatens to obliterate selfhood. Earlier the beautiful apparition of Mahalia Jackson excited the poet to limn her appearance with lyric citations, garlanding the singer, but also protecting her by linking her to other histories. Here in the nursing home the superfluity of "sadness," which threatens to overwhelm both the speaker and the value of the word, is brought back to meaning by the poet's recollection of the word's meanings—which, despite her claim that "once it meant something real," turns out to have meant many contradictory things. If the arraying of citations allows Rankine to participate in shared or otherwise dispersed vulnerabilities, this glossing of definitions allows her momentarily to restore herself to contradiction and multiplicity—to be "dignified" and "shameful," to be "trustworthy" and "dark." Rankine's paraphrase of the dot-com era's existential question—"to eTrade or not to eTrade?"—pointed to a sham "individuation" based on everyone becoming a stakeholder, a form of sharing risk that meant, not sharing, but enmeshment and catastrophe. But in her turn to the dictionary, to the moment of becoming literate, she reconceives the order of texts as a medium for the mutuality that risk-sharing, securitization, mocks: linked vulnerability.

Ramifying Capital: Kevin Davies

If for Rankine the scene of contemporary poetry is the imaginary confrontation of a television with the dictionary, or the news with a scrapbook, for Kevin Davies it's the collision of the Internet with argument, especially what he calls "lateral argument"—a rhetorical style in which lists, and cross-referenced links, mimic the laterality of a network that dwarfs poetry. For Rankine, the science-fiction action blockbuster becoming a spectacle signaled what in some sense she already knew, that "salvation narratives are passé"; for Davies, contemporary social relations give the lie to historical hope, especially as they are enmeshed in production processes—here, the production of computer technology:

> *The world / / to come has come and gone, Ed.* Do you have any idea how cheap memory
>   is now?
>
> (20–21)

This "cheapness" of "memory" allows for kinds of laterality, Davies suggests, that operate as the cutting edge of social enclosure even as they mimic older forms of argument. Here is a key portion of the poem "Lateral Argument":

> Any surface at all, inside or out, you touch it
>   and a scrolled menu appears, listing recent history,
> chemical makeup, distance to the sun in millimetres,
>   distance to the Vatican in inches, famous people
> who have previously touched this spot, fat content,
>   will to power, adjacencies, and further articulations.
> And each category has dozens of subcategories
>   and each subcategory scores of its own, all
> meticulously cross-referenced, *linked,* so that each square
>   centimetre of surface everywhere, pole to pole,
> from the top of the mightiest Portuguese bell tower to
>   the intestinal lining of a sea turtle off Ecuador, has
> billions of words and images attached, and a special area,
>   *a little rectangle,* for you to add your own comments.
> It is the great work of a young-adult global
>   civilization, a metaliterate culture with time on its
> prosthetic tentacles, at this point slightly more silicon

than carbon, blinking vulnerably in the light of its own
radiant connectedness.

(58)

This description of "metaliterate culture" is both science-fictionally futuristic—data lining the walls of intestines—and emphatically scholastic: "each category has dozens of subcategories." Indeed, "metaliteracy" in this passage seems to describe the subsumption and retooling of older forms of capturing data, at least analogically: the Internet is like an extended, intensified system of scholia.

Indeed, there is a postcatastrophic monasticism in the background of Davies' work, as when he writes, "[Illegible] swoon, asteroids / / collide / with protocurrency" (130–131; slash marks mine; brackets original to poem; double brackets indicate a page break). In a short passage like this, the implied scene is the library, or the scriptorium, where monks take down the last fainting records of capitalist apocalypse from within the chaos of its aftermath. Elsewhere he slyly entertains a Buddhist monasticism, too: "At the age of two I attained my cat / and then she was // gone: lesson" (38). Together these two monkishnesses mark out the great concern of Davies' poetry, which, I hope to show, involves the twining together of a cosmological interest in the appearance of matter in the universe with a rhetorician's concern for making a counterargument to the "argument" of matter's arrangement by capital.

Now of course the roles of monk, scholastic, and rhetorician are hardly the same, though at different times and places they may have overlapped. But aspects of all of them are at play as imaginary positions in Davies' writing, which to my mind has reached an extraordinary pitch in his most recent book, *The Golden Age of Paraphernalia* (2008). So in what follows I would like to track something like the textual imaginary of this book, which labors to develop textual forms that capture the meeting between matter becoming a thing and its social organization. In addressing this concern I think Davies has written the most powerful account of—and argument against—contemporary capitalism in English-language poetry.

The Golden Age of Paraphernalia is built around five overlapping poems, two of which ("'Floater'" and "Remnants of Wilma") are identified in the book by the marks he uses to break up them up—a bullet point and a vertical slash. A third poem ("One-Eyed Seller of Garlic") is written as a numbered sequence; two others ("Lateral Argument" and "Duckwalking a Perimeter") interrupt the first three for twenty-six and thirteen pages, respectively. Parts of the bullet-point and vertical-slash poems frequently appear on the same page; the numbered sequence, though continually interrupted by the first two poems, is always the only kind of poem on the pages where it appears. Though the book contains several references to aleatory composition, by and large the different poems make no real invitation to be read as though they should be fortuitously connected by the reader—given their strong syntactical continuity, one finds that the best way to read the book is to skip back and forth among them until distraction or the allure of an adjacent sequence compels jumping to a different poem. The system of the book is clear, that is, but one reads it with a drifting relation to that system.

Meanwhile, at the level of the line, sentence, and phrase, Davies makes brilliant use of italics and small caps to indicate rueful and hilarious forms of amazement, dismay, outrage, and a kind of speech-from-elsewhere that seems to mime interpellation by some superstate or other apparatus. In the portion of "Lateral Argument" I cited above, for instance, the italics for "*linked,*" "*a little rectangle,*" and "*radiant connectedness*" convey the observer's fascinated horror at the depth of the data-scholasticism he sees; they act as a kind of meta-measurement to the repeated uses of words like "centimetres," "millimetres," "dozens, and "billions"—they mark the conversion point from quantity to quality. The small caps, meanwhile, tend to mark language that feels visited on the poems. They make most sense in relation to what's around them; take, for instance, the first page of the book:

Elected will be *a thin strip of tungsten*
Bothered by rumours of
Foreign birth • Cold snap—
old shoes. • THE REMAINS
TO BE SEEN. • Something
put in the gas
to make the air better
has made the water worse.
Tumours in
rats • But

(1)

Elsewhere the small caps mark first-person speech that feels helplessly amplified, or postcatastrophic: "I AM BURNING / MY BURKA AND SHAVING MY BEARD" (127)—or, more pointedly, on this page:

laundry Canadiana • The e-mail sublime—live turtles
in the fibre optics
swimming toward Hull • I AM SITTING
IN A ROOM THREE BLOCKS AWAY
LISTENING TO ALVIN LUCIER
AND READING A FINANCIAL DOCUMENT
when the first plane hits the
tower • *Place*

(9)

The small caps, which reference Lucier's 1969 sound piece "I Am Sitting in a Room," help establish their rhetorical function, which, a bit like that of the poems' italics, is at least partly to mark the place where catastrophe or extremity pushes speech close to something like mere element, or item. Lucier's eight-minute piece involved his recording his voice describing his aims for making the recording, and then recording the recording, over and over, until by the last repetition the contours of his words are lost—until, as he puts it, "what you will hear . . . are the natural resonant frequencies of the room articulated by speech."

If Davies' small-cap lines make early and illuminating reference to a scene of speech becoming sound, the bullet points and vertical bars that separate shorter sections of the poem highlight something slightly different, something like the subsumption of poetry by software, or the poetic line by the line of code. The bullet point, of course, is most familiar to us since the 1990s as a marker for listed items in Microsoft's PowerPoint, which has long been an object of criticism and satire for how it seems to make its users begin to think in lists, subsuming meaning to the program's form (Tufte, *Cognitive Style of PowerPoint*). As for Davies' use of the vertical bar, Joshua Clover has pointed out that it not only serves as the traditional mathematical marker of absolute value (so that |3|, say, is the absolute value of both +3 and -3), but as the "pipe" or command marker in UNIX, routing, organizing, or transforming information from one side of the bar to functions or destinations on the other side (Clover, *Autumn of the System*).

Words and phrases as data; words and phrases whose positive or negative valence are made secondary to the mere fact of their being pieces of language; language becoming mere sound: all these effects combine with the page-to-page drift and skipping created by the overlap of the book's poems to create a kind of "argument" in which poetic language is pushed toward becoming a list, becoming a command, becoming a schematic—toward losing aesthetic power and literary specificity. But these effects are not designed to be part of an anti-aesthetic program, I don't think—Davies' whip-smart satire and the sheer typographic beauty of his pages argue emphatically enough against that. I think, rather, that Davies wants to push poetic language toward becoming mere linguistic stuff in order better to understand how it comes into the world at all. Recall the first line of the book, "Elected will be *a thin strip of tungsten,*" whose verb tense places us in the before-and-after of the scene of "election," creating a kind of empty space around the uncapturable present by highlighting the moment before and the moment after. In this case that arrival-in-the-world is partly what the italics are meant to emphasize—the sheer thingness of the "thin strip." This feels like part of what I referred to before as the book's cosmological impulse—Davies uses the word "universe" many times in *Golden Age*—and it is linked to other, terrified but fascinated inquiries like this one, harrowing in its simplicity: "*What is inaugurated?*" (5). Both the word "election" and the word "inauguration" make notice of the controversies around elections during the Bush II years, of course, and I will return to this below; but I'd like to pause for a moment to think about another facet of Davies' sense of his poems as "argument."

At one point in the poem "Lateral Argument" Davies writes, "I take comfort in histories of education / and their attendant heartbreaks." Actually those lines feel like part of a fuller three-line passage:

> I don't have a biography, I'm lower
> middle-class. I take comfort in histories of education
> And their attendant heartbreaks.
>
> (60)

Part of what it means to make an "argument," for Davies, is to make oneself legible in class-specific terms, in rhetorics that must be laboriously acquired, and whose acquisition he experiences as an encounter with power. Davies' 2000 volume, in fact, is called *Comp.*, short for "Composition"—famously the subject that serves as a teaching mill for part-time or nontenured literary-academic workers, and as the front line in the last stages of making young adults fully "literate." Davies puts it this way in a poem from that volume:

> I learned the year after kindergarten that sentences
> are linguistic artifacts with regulations that fill them-

selves out, and that for the purposes of our circus-cannon
ambitions the most important part of the war they enact
is the full-stopping dots that divide the booty amongst
camp-following berserkers of the sub-syllabic frontier. Word.

(Comp., 33)

What counts as a "sentence," then, gets to count as such only by way of pedagogical processes likened, not only to "war," here, and the hunt for "booty," but to absurd, comical, and possibly self-mutilating "ambitions," as in being shot out of a cannon. The "sentence" becomes literary matter only at the cost of these forms of violence, then, while the pupil, the object of this booty-pedagogy, seems willing to climb into a cannon because of the implicit promise that literacy will make up for the absence of biography. In a class sense, then, the lower-middle-class pupil "comes from nowhere" in the way that matter, for Davies, seems to "come from nowhere," cosmologically.

The "heartbreak," here, of dubious educational promises made to those with no high origins, recalls Auden's elegy for Louis MacNeice, where he writes:

For Grammar we both inherited
  good mongrel barbarian English
which never completely succumbed to the Roman rhetoric
  or the Roman gravity, that nonsense
which stood none. Though neither of our dads, like Horace's,
  wiped his nose on his forearm,
neither was porphyry-born, and our ancestors probably
  were among those plentiful subjects
it cost less money to murder.

(*Selected Poems*, 692)

Indeed, in a passage from the numbered "One Eyed Seller of Garlic" poem in *Golden Age*, Davies echoes this passage of Auden's even more emphatically:

The statistical certainty:
  at least one of one's ancestors
      sacrificed in a religious rite
Scarcity
  made us,
     look it up!

(80–81)

For Auden, a useable literacy develops out of a "barbarian" resistance to Latinity that he thinks is built into English; for Davies, the barbarians are the "berserker" pedagogues, Old Norse plunderers of language's raw material ("the sub-syllabic frontier"). In Auden's case, as we saw, the appropriate literary comportment is a kind of purgatorial or postcatastrophic middle style, a kind of campy *sermo humilis* always signaling its awareness of the absurdity of humble creatures speaking into scenes of disaster far vaster than themselves, disasters they've created through the unleashing of their own collective force. For Davies, the comportment that grows out of his sense of where literacy comes from is something like a continuation of English-language literary modernism, especially in the Poundian, juxtapositional vein. This modernism provides a kind of alternative literacy to the one garnered in the "[history] of education," and Davies links himself to it even as he marks it as inadequate to the violence of class relations. That is, he most often cites it to mock it:

• YES, I
TOO "CONTINUED ON" TO COLLEGE, HOWEVER,
[two-page break]
THE PHILADELPHIA RIOTS OF 1843.
I PARKED A CAR
IN TENNESSEE, •

(14, 16)

These lines, of course, reference Wallace Stevens's "Anecdote of the Jar," a poem about how arrangement, placement, seems to induce materiality—in this case, landscape—into being:

I placed a jar in Tennessee,
And round it was, upon a hill.
It made the slovenly wilderness
Surround that hill.

(Stevens, *Collected Poems*, 76)

The metaphysics of Stevens's poem are both whimsical and high-literary: the world induces itself around the poet's emplacement of the humble object, which action makes a bid for literary imagination as the arbiter of reality. Davies' rhyming rewrite—"car" for "jar," and, in his own poem, "1843" with "Tennessee"—keeps faith with the playful simplicity of Stevens's original, which is also built around easy rhymes. But the context in which

Davies' lines are set darkens the parody: "YES, I TOO 'CONTINUED ON' TO COLLEGE, HOWEVER, / / THE PHILADELPHIA RIOTS OF 1843." Those anti-Catholic, anti-Irish riots, Davies implies, are part of the heritage of the flank of the "lower / middle class" of which he forms a part, and they make high modernism a strange, polemical choice of vehicle for the counterliteracy the poet wants to cultivate.

But then English-language literary modernism was itself polemical, not least in its Poundian form. Davies makes a link to Pound explicitly, both by concluding the first of his numbered poems with the same inaugurating phrase that ends the first of The Cantos, "So that:"—and by referencing Canto XXXVIII at least twice in *Golden Age,* that Canto being the place where Pound most clearly lays out his "A + B" economic theory. Pound again:

A factory
has also another aspect, which we call the financial aspect
It gives people the power to buy (wages, dividends
which are power to buy) but it is also the cause of prices
or values, financial, I mean financial values
. . .
and the power to purchase can never
(under the present system) catch up with
prices at large,
        and the light became so bright and so blindin'
in this layer of paradise
    that the mind of man was bewildered.

(The Cantos, 190)

Davies sees this "A + B" theory as exactly what keeps Pound from fulfilling his ambition to make the Cantos cohere:

| Let's hold
this initial long shot of Pound first presenting himself to
Mussolini | *Later*
    close-ups of respectively rapt and *bemused* attention |
    Pound's
uncharacteristic mistakes, nervous, in spoken Italian,
[two-page break]
    marches drained by then? And which are? | And the
    consequences

being? | It's
simple | The system
starts to malfunction
about halfway through the composition | This is an accident
of *piety:*
[page break]
can be looked up
to | A fairy princess
In-a-box, A + B
cannot buy enough to propel the economy
into a renaissance of Ruskinian objects appreciated on days
off

(128, 130–131)

Pound's Cantos begin with a scene of pious sacrifice, the scene of Aeneas sacrificing animals to the gods so as to be able to speak to his mother in the underworld. Inasmuch as Davies sees the "malfunction" of the "composition" of the Cantos as "an accident of piety," then, he is implying a link between an ancestral piety driven by sacrifice and an economic theory that sees only blocked liquidity (Pound's "power to purchase"), and not exploitation, as the problem. You might say it's the difference between a poet who uses the figure of pious sacrifice to the ancestors as a metaphor for his relation to the literary past, and a poet who imagines his ancestors as having *been* sacrificed in the name of "piety."

One such ancestor of Davies', it seems to me, is Petrus Ramus, the sixteenth-century rhetorician and educator, murdered in Paris during the anti-Protestant riots on St. Bartholomew's Day of 1572, and a key figure in what Davies would call the "history of education," with its "attendant heartbreak." Indeed, it is hard to hear the phrase "lateral argument" and *not* think of Ramus, whose diagrammatic teaching method became widely influential in England and western Europe, and whose spatializing of argument is arguably an important precursor of the kind of spatialization of thought we hear critiqued today in the objections to the spread of PowerPoint. The image we have today of Ramist "argument," in fact, is a diagrammed page whose "laterality" is developed around the forking apart of "dichotomies."

This dichotomizing, diagramming method, though undeniably influential, has a confusing role in intellectual history, because it justified itself in philosophical terms, as a critique of the messiness of scholasticism; but it is a method more than a philosophy, so its influence was felt in earlier levels of education than in the university, where philosophical history largely takes place. The title of the definitive English-language study of Ramus, Walter Ong's *Ramus: Method, and the Decay of Dialogue,* names exactly the issue—Ramism was a method, not a philosophy, but because it was a *pedagogical* method, it fought for position alongside philosophy, and against older, dialectical forms of university education, even though its main locus of influence, as I say, was in pre-university education. For Ong, Ramism has no philosophical legitimacy, but it gained unfortunate post facto cachet because it helped prepare the ground for later, spatializing theories of the universe and of the mind, as with Newton and Descartes (*Ramus,* 164–164, 318). As Ong puts it:

> The hypertrophy of the visual imagination which we observe [in seventeenth-century Ramist diagramming of argument]—a hypertrophy extraordinarily striking in the way it crowds spatial models, and nothing but spatial models, into the universe of the mind—is in another way witness to the evolution in human thought processes which is simultaneously producing the Newtonian revolution, with its stress on visually controlled observation and mathematics, and its curiously silent, nonrhetorical universe. (318)

That last word—"universe"—highlights what Ong suggests was a felt connection, in the sixteenth and seventeenth centuries, between argumentative schematization and the arrangement of the material world—or, as he puts it, the "universe of physics" and the "universe of the mind" (318). Work like Davies' makes it possible to sense that, even in the twenty-first century, a certain argumentative impulse to the "lateral," to the "diagrammatic," implicitly calls up the rhetorical, educational, and intellectual histories in which "the universe" and "the mind" were intertwined.

This historical relationship extends, Ong shows, even to component elements of print culture, like typesetting and typefaces. He details the analogies by which fifteenth-century humanists linked the production of movable type to the production of argument, and the elements of type to the "loci" or "places" out of which arguments were built: "This reduction of the elements of intelligibility to the spatial arrangements of printing of the topical logics suggests a further general theorem: the printer's font corresponds to the locus of the topical logics, and the printed page to methodized discourse" (310).

What's lost, for Ong, in arguments having become spatialized, and the focus on method in humanism, is a bulwark against the "decay of dialogue," the older teacher-student relationships that once organized university life. He opposes what he calls, in his later *Orality and Literacy,* "the technologizing of the word." And he blames Ramus for helping facilitate this technologization—*Ramus* is extraordinary for how Ong's meticulous and indispensable research on Ramus is paired with a continuous disdain for his work.

Davies, meanwhile, takes up the Ramist tradition, including making "argument" methodical by the deployment of schematization and of varied typefaces, to pit his poems, not against a "technologization" per se, but against the social relationships out of which that technologization has grown. One way to track those relationships, for Davies, is to probe the extent and intensity of capitalism's reorganization of material life, right down to the production of quiddity itself. Early in *Comp.,* he uses italics to rewrite Marx's famous lines from the "Theses on Feuerbach": where the original reads "The philosophers have only *interpreted* the world, in various ways; the point, however, is to *change* it," Davies writes, "The point, however, is to change *it*" (19). The italics are an attempt to seize on it-ness, whose capture Davies names as the fluctuating and perpetual project of surplus extraction—evident, he suggests, even in the arrival of material in the world: "Class violence at the level of the seedling" (19).

So Davies takes up the tools of schematizing rhetoric to bat back the capture of the material world by capital, knowing full well how bivalent, unstable, and minor those tools are. This rhetoric, after all, is either an aspect of the extension of class power—"berzerkers of the sub-syllabic frontier"—or a means of bringing literacy to the less elite, that is, those who will never make it to the university level, where rhetoric might once again be dialogic rather than schematic ("I take comfort in histories of education / and their attendant heartbreaks"). Part of the power of Davies' poetry is that, in taking up the techniques of schematization and reworking them to his purposes, he becomes capable of telling historical time even in hell—if hell is the place where there is no horizon, no limit to what can be made to *work.* Look at the Inferno that concludes "Lateral Argument," where the italics mark both the speech of power, its ability to name every "thing," and the pathetic counterefforts of the aesthetic, whose "arguments," reduced to mere naked assertion, do nothing to stop the madness:

> It is a *fecund and holy thing,* this announcement paid for
> by the Patriarchy in Action Committee to Reelect
> a Chunk of Wood. Summer dwindles into X.
> The young graphic artists and web designers stand on street corners
> hoping for day labor, next to hookers slugging forties.
> Most of the crops look bad, the reservoirs are severely
> depleted, and a huge brown
> cloud hangs over south Asia.
> The very fact that *you are writing*
> *a string quartet* is itself an argument.
> I then witnessed my own liver being roasted.
>
> (61)

As with Rankine, the bubble has become the crash, and posthistorical network has collapsed back into "day labor." But it's worse: nature creeps toward disaster, and the subject of the aesthetic jots down notes while Rome burns—indeed, while Rome burns *him.*

In this gesture Davies joins the array of English-language poets who, in the American century, linked the political minority of poets and poetry to the techniques of print or textual humanism to stage a counterargument to capital, or to stave it off, or to camouflage the poetic in the face of it. In his sense of the David-and-Goliath absurdity of the subjects of capital trying to address its might, he is probably closest to the Auden, who, in "Caliban to the Audience," mangles speech to highlight the ridiculousness of the low trying to speak in the idiom of the high. But it's not a question of style, for Davies. The end of "Lateral Argument" is closer to the end of Michael Palmer's "Sun," where the fire-writing of napalmed Vietnamese villages seems like a wavering, agentless prophecy of the end of American hegemony at the moment of its consolidation: "The writing occurs on their walls." Even Palmer's dark agnostic prophecy, though, had behind it a generation of antiwar activism to tilt the austerity of the line in the direction of historical reckoning; it's not clear to what constituency, in the late-Bush ("Chunk of Wood") or early Obama years, the poetry speaks. At least that's true in political terms; perhaps, in his emphasis on the power and the powerlessness that emerges from the pedagogies of "argument," the constituency Davies imagines is less a generation of activists than a generation of text or code workers, who've learned to argue, to handle text, to learn to be willing to be fired out of a cannon if it will keep the peace. The latest crash has made the handlers of texts into "day labor"; they are, if nothing else, more aware of the value of their time. That hardly makes for a prophetic turn; but it does refresh a sense that the tools of argument, its materials, its gestures, are just that, tools:

> These cheesy little hypertexts
> are going to get better.
> I don't know
> how *much* better, but *we'll see.*
>
> (Comp., 67)

Notes

Bibliography

Acknowledgments

Index

Notes

Introduction

1. The classic review of Arthurian "matter" is Roger Sherman Loomis, *The Development of Arthurian Romance* (Norton, 1970). For recent scholarship on "the matter of France," see Gabriele and Stuckey. I am grateful to Seeta Chaganti for this recommendation.
2. See Curtius, *European Literature and the Latin Middle Ages.* Curtius's history of the different topoi by which poets depicted the character of poetry, and their social role as poets, has been an indispensable model for my exploration of how poetry imagines itself in relation to capital.
3. See, crucially, Nelson's *Revolutionary Memory: Recovering the Poetry of the American Left* (Routledge, 2001), which not only helped restore to visibility the poetry of individual writers like Tillie Olsen and Edwin Rolfe, but also made clear that in the 1930s there was for American poets on the left something like a "Matter of Spain"—that is, a body of work devoted to hashing out the meanings of support for the antifascist cause during the Spanish Civil War.
4. The contours of the American discourse of the critique of "totalization" would make for an entire book; arguably, Martin Jay's splendid *Marxism and Totality* would be its prequel. In any case the best current example of this argument is probably to be found in the work of the philosopher Jacques Rancière, who, for instance, described his work this way in a 2007 interview:

   > What interests me more than politics or art is the way the boundaries defining certain practices as artistic or political are drawn and redrawn. This frees artistic and political creativity from the yoke of the great historical schemata that announce the great revolutions to come or that mourn the great revolutions past only to impose their proscriptions and their declarations of powerlessness on the present. (Rancière, *ArtForum,* March 2007)

   Again, notice that it is Marxist theory, not capitalism, that oppresses.

5. Kristeva makes fascinating use of Freud's account of the "binding" of excitation in the work of managing the death drive in her account of the negativity of the best modern poetry, which, like Derrida's Bataille, smashes through negativity's mere "amortization":

> This would seem to be "art'"s function as a signifying practice: under the pleasing exterior of a very socially acceptable differentiation, art reintroduces into society fundamental rejection, which is matter in the process of splitting. (*Revolution in Poetic Language,* 180)

Nancy, whose citation from Bataille analogizes the wrong role for literature to the work of Party officials ("the task of directing collective necessity"), rereads Marx as a theorist, not of the sham "communism" that is merely state-directed capitalism, but of multiform, inorganic "articulation" or assemblage—a practice that looks a lot like modernist collage:

> It is not an exaggeration to say that Marx's community is, in this sense, a community of literature—or at least it opens on to such a community. It is a community of articulation, not organization, and precisely because of this it is a community situated "beyond the sphere of material production properly speaking," where "begins the flowering of that human power that is its own end, the true reign of liberty. (*The Inoperable Community,* 77)

6. I am grateful to Joshua Clover for first pointing out to me the disproportionate amount of critical energy spent on this small canon of poets. See Clover, "A Form Adequate to History."
7. See Erich Auerbach, *Literary Language and Its Public.* For Adorno's argument, see "Lyric Poetry and Society."
8. I am indebted to the critic Margaret Ronda for her insights into the importance of questions of framing and medium-sensitivity in Rukeyser's documentary poetic practice. See Ronda, *Disenchanted Georgics.*
9. See Baker, *Blues, Ideology, and Afro-American Literature.*
10. For a concise history of environmental politics since World War II, see Bramwell, *The Fading of the Greens.* For two very different accounts of how this history has inflected literary criticism, see Buell, *The Environmental Imagination,* and Fletcher, *A New Theory for American Poetry.*
11. Ransom's poem begins:

> Garrulous gentlemen on a verandah,
> Bibbers or non-bibbers of illicit potations,
> Rehearsing the acta and the agenda
> Of Republican or Democratic administrations,
> I am not committed to taking memoranda
> Culled from the lacunae of your cerebrations

Despite his elaborate Latinity, he positions himself more as Caliban than as Promethean hero: "I attend you as some tired jungle monster."

1. A Method and a Tone

1. Duncan, for instance, shocked his literary peers by coming out of the closet in a 1944 essay, "The Homosexual in Society," in Dwight MacDonald's *Politics* magazine; and Spicer worked intensively with the Mattachine Society in Oakland to develop a framework for lesbian and gay organizing. For a detailed account of Spicer's political work, see Kevin Killian, "Spicer and The Mattachine," forthcoming in John Emil Vincent, *After Spicer.*
2. On Pound's regrets, see Redman. It is worth noting that Leon Surette, another key scholar of Pound's economic theories, finds those regrets insignificant compared to the building intensity, and sheer insistence, of Pound's anti-Semitism after about 1936 (see Surette, *Pound in Purgatory*). Auden's later views on his youthful leftism, and his excision from his body of work of what he took to be programmatic leftist writing, have been widely acknowledged; the most concise précis of Auden's actions and attitude are to be found in Edward Mendelson, *Early Auden.*
3. There are many informative studies of how the shift in the link between leftist politics and its cultural and aesthetic expressions was enacted and perceived after the 1930s. I have found the following especially helpful: Judy Kutulas, *The Long War,* especially chapter 8; and Cary Nelson, *Repression and Recovery.*
4. Again, there is a wide-ranging literature on the twentieth-century link between political liberalism in its broadest sense, as a theory of the centrality of the individual (and not the class, or the mass) to politics, and consumer-driven capitalism. From the angle of global history, Eric Hobsbawm's *The Age of Extremes* is especially useful, not least for the way Hobsbawm keeps the impact of the Russian Revolution, and the existence of a wide noncapitalist world, in view as he discusses the interwar period. This emphasis allows Hobsbawm to highlight the negative aspect of capitalism's self-definition in the twentieth century, that is, its constant positioning as a better alternative to communism. A key American history of the later part of this period is Walter LaFeber's *America, Russia, and the Cold War, 1945–2006,* which has gone through ten editions since its first publication in 1972, and which stresses the decisions of policy makers in this period to stage capitalism and communism as fatally opposed. By 1976, meanwhile, Daniel Bell had already produced a comprehensive sociology of the links among politics, economics, and culture from early to mid-twentieth century, in *The Cultural Contradictions of Capitalism,* which read the "contradictions" of liberal capitalist culture through the lens of the tension between individual desires and collective social organization. And the literary-critical tradition of thinking through literature's significance to liberal political ideals (and, implicitly, to the capitalist social arrangements that subtend them) dates at least to the work of the New York Intellectuals,

congealing perhaps most succinctly in Lionel Trilling's *The Liberal Imagination* of 1950. Central among the many more recent studies of the work of literature in critiquing (rather than buttressing) liberal-capitalist personhood is Michael Denning's *The Cultural Front,* which emphasizes how the tendency of capitalism toward crisis kept alive a set of alternative visions even in the postwar era, when they seemed least articulate. This emphasis on crisis is thought through carefully in Michael Szalay's *New Deal Modernism,* which reads the production and consumption of literature as mediating "a tension between liberal agency on the one hand, and collectivizing, compensatory strategies of risk management on the other" (5). As for economic histories accessible to the lay reader, I find indispensable Harry Shutt's *The Trouble with Capitalism,* not least for its flexible but analytically clear understanding of crisis as the structural instability of global capitalism, and its perpetual need for stabilization—an emphasis of use for the literary critic who is trying to understand a pervasive sense of "crisis" in the work of writers who cannot or do not specify an actual, punctual "crisis" in their writing.

5. Elsewhere in *The Age of Extremes,* Hobsbawm describes the troubles of representative democracy in the interwar years this way: "at bottom liberal politics was vulnerable because its characteristic form of government, representative democracy, was rarely a convincing way of running states, and the conditions of the Age of Catastrophe rarely guaranteed the conditions that made it viable" (138). On the language of "liquidation" in the interwar period, see Beaud 184.
6. On the problem that the apparent viability of Soviet-style communism posed for the capitalist nations (and capitalist classes), see Hobsbawm, chapters 2 through 5; and Shutt, chapter 1.
7. Surette's *Pound in Purgatory* makes clear that Pound's anti-Semitism drew force from his understanding of the workings of economics—and therefore of history—as a conspiracy, which blinded Pound to the possibility that economies generate structures, and causal forms, other than those of the cabal. Also extremely helpful to me has been Richard Sieburth's "In Pound We Trust: The Economy of Poetry / The Poetry of Economics," which explores the implications of the link between Pound's notion of successful economies as efficient engines of distribution, on the one hand, and of good poetry as efficiently arranged, on the other. Tim Redman's essay "Pound's Politics and Economics" helpfully sketches the similarities and differences between the monetary lens through which Pound viewed economics and the later monetarist theories that, through Keynes, came to influence the economics of the period from 1945 to 1973. Finally, Maud Ellman's "Ezra Pound: The Erasure of History" offers a brilliant tour of the sexual, bodily, and historiographical valences of 'usury' in *The Cantos,* including a sharp gloss on Pound's distaste for the dialectic, which he felt did not do justice to the movement of history,

which could be obscured and derailed from its right course, but never produced out of contradiction. See Ellman in Attridge, Bennington, and Young.

8. See Bernstein, *The Tale of The Tribe.* Bernstein's book remains exemplary for its focus on how *The Cantos* got away from Pound, how the emerging impossibility of making them a unified object with an overriding theme altered, over the fifty years of the poem's composition, the meaning and the deployment of its techniques: fragmentation, for instance, beginning as a strategy for illuminating a hidden truth, but gradually becoming a form of grasping after that truth's receding horizon.
9. Pound's resentment of this style of teaching is by no means idiosyncratic—indeed, it is practically exemplary of how young men and women of the late nineteenth and early twentieth centuries felt about the grammatically driven approach to the classics. As Gerald Graff writes, "In most cases . . . the chief result of the classical drill work [in the colleges of the second half of the nineteenth century] was to imbue the student with a lifelong hatred of classical languages." See Graff, *Professing Literature,* 31.
10. Marc Shell has argued that most postclassical rhetorical theorists, when they discuss the value of literary "economy," are drifting, "as if by a bad metaphor," from the sense in which Aristotle first used "economy." Aristotle, Shell argues, used the word in a socially grounded way, so that "bad economy" in a play implied the depiction of households *(oikoi)* of an inappropriate social level for their genre—the depiction of middle-born households as material for tragedy, for instance. For Shell, every use of "economy" as a literary value since Aristotle has fallen away from this social specificity, branching, in the Latin world, into *dispositio*—the arrangement of a text's parts—and dispensation, the question of cultural husbandry and literary circulation of which the production of texts forms a part. Only *dispositio,* Shell argues, survives as the meaning of literary "economy," leaving the other half of the original Aristotelian formulation, a text's dispensation, unexamined (*The Economy of Literature,* 90–102). Halpern's book goes a long way toward explaining why it is not simply a "bad metaphor," but a set of social processes, that leads to the forgetting of dispensation in discussions of literary economy. Pound's project is aimed against this forgetting, and its failure—that is, the failure of the poem to induce the form of social organization it advocates for—is a testament to the separation of *dispositio* and dispensation as more than just a linguistic problem, or a problem of how literary critics practice interpretation.
11. Here is the relevant passage:

> [The ancient mind] did indeed divide human nature into its several aspects, and project these in magnified form into the divinities of its glorious pantheon; but not by tearing it to pieces; rather by combining its aspects in different proportions, for in no single one of their deities was humanity in

> its entirety ever lacking. How different with us Moderns! With us too the image of the human species is projected in magnified form into separate individuals—but as fragments, not in different combinations, with the result that one has to go the rounds from one individual to another in order to be able to piece together a complete image of the species.

12. Indeed, that cheeky poem is a good measure of what Auden would attempt in his longer work of the late 1930s, which was to coordinate a sense of modernity as the scene of historical catastrophe with camp disruptions of style level, and to highlight the role of literature-at-large in mediating fragmented relations between single poems and the textual systems in which they circulate. Written in the seven-line stanza of Chaucer's rhyme royal, A-B-A-B-B-C-C, the poem is framed as the low addressing the high—"Excuse, my Lord, the liberty I take / In thus addressing you"—and it begins with a series of literary abasements, not least Auden's insistence that "novel writing is / A higher art then poetry altogether" (he was going to write to Jane Austen, he tells Byron, but the thought was too intimidating). So he turns to Byron—a Lord, yes, but lambasted as middle-brow, and like Auden, "master of the airy manner." Auden defends Byron against his critics, concluding: "only on a varied diet can we live," he writes: "The pious fable and the dirty story / Share in the total literary glory."
13. Murphy defends the poem against Randall Jarell's dismissal of it on the grounds that it was a retreat from modernist innovation; Murphy suggests, at the close of his essay, that in fact the poem is an attempt to dialectically recuperate an older form, the epistle, for the purposes of confronting the problems for poetry posed by "late modernity."

2. John Ashbery's Optional Apocalypse

1. At least two generations of critics have held to this view of Ashbery, most obviously Marjorie Perloff, who aligns him with a tradition of "indeterminacy" *(Poetics of Indeterminacy).* Charles Altieri has a similarly epistemological view, reading Ashbery as reflecting primarily on the capacities of the imagination in relation to knowledge. As he puts it:

> Poetry for Ashbery is the art that makes the importance of "now" in writing visible and lasting, primarily by staging the force of that sense of presence against various elements that threaten it, like "certitude." (*The Art of Twentieth-Century American Poetry,* 212)

These epistemologically driven readings of Ashbery are often paired with observations that if his poems are ultimately about what we can and cannot know, they are also therefore about the specific character of language as a medium—or philosophy's understanding of that specificity: a recent essay by Nick Lolordo, which very succinctly traces the recent history of Ashbery criticism, concludes this way, arguing that Ashbery's language "[preserves] the surprise, the otherness of language and the nonidentity of our words and selves" ("Charting the Flow," 770).

2. These political and financial transformations of New York have a longer history, of course, but even if we only look back a decade or so, we can see that artists had already begun to take note of them. Especially noteworthy is the emergence of an object-oriented visual art in the 1960s, which the art historian Joshua Shannon has persuasively argued forms a response to the great wave of infrastructural regularization and cleanup we identify with the work of Robert Moses. If Moses's philosophy of urbanism is accurately reflected in his famous statement that "cities are created by and for traffic," the artists Shannon studies clearly felt that the city was for detritus. Robert Rauschenberg's "combines" of the sixties, hybrids of painting and sculpture crammed with pieces of furniture, newspaper clippings, and stuffed birds—and Claes Oldenburg's early found-object environments like *The Street* and *The Store* (from 1959 and 1961, respectively) filled with stray objects and craft imitations of real commodities—tried to stall or capture Moses's relentless "traffic," to keep it on a human scale (Shannon, *Disappearance of Objects;* Dunn and Hood, *New York: The Unknown City*). This human messiness and intricacy was already being aggressively regularized by the late 1950s—indeed, this period gives form to the first great critique of top-down "urban renewal," Jane Jacobs's *The Death and Life of Great American Cities* of 1961.
3. All page references to Ashbery's poems in the following paragraphs are to his *Collected Poems, 1956–1987.*

3. "Language" in Spicer and After

1. Spicer's interest in making an analogy between poetry and "language," as midcentury linguistics understood it, meant, in the first wave of Spicer scholarship after the poet's death, a close attention to Spicer's relationship to "language" in a poststructuralist sense: see especially the essays collected in the Autumn 1977 issue of *boundary 2.* For an incisive overview of early Spicer criticism, see Vincent, "Before *After Spicer.*"
2. This isn't Spicer's first use of the "Turkish bath" figure in his correspondence. In a 1958 letter to Robin Blaser in which he describes why he sees serial forms as an advance over his earlier practice of writing stand-alone lyrics, he writes:

   > That is why all my stuff from the past (except the *Elegies* and *Troilus*) looks foul to me. The poems belong nowhere. They are one night stands filled (the best of them) with their own emotions, but pointing nowhere, as meaningless as sex in a Turkish bath. (Blaser 61)

In the letter to Persky, the Turkish bath is a scene of overfamiliarity; here it is a figure for lonely anonymity. But in both cases it is an index of the relation of poetic practice to the use of the name: both first-name only and anonymous contexts are implicitly devalued in relation to the medium—print, but also poetry—where one makes use of a full name.

3. Spicer led an actual picket of one of Duncan's plays, which Spicer thought uninspired and seemed to think of as having drifted too far from the barroom sociability he felt was poetry's true source. Spicer also antagonized other members of the Bay Area poetry scene, like Lawrence Ferlinghetti, whom Spicer considered a sellout for purchasing the anarchist City Lights Books, and goaded poets not to take the route of reading for money. Ellingham and Killian tell a story of Spicer, having been told that the poet Philip Whalen was going to be paid $10 to read at a poetry festival, saying "I'll offer him $11 not to read" (*Poet Be Like God,* 228, 240).
4. See also the correspondence reproduced in *Manroot* number 10 (1974–1975).
5. Invention and alchemy—perhaps this is why Spicer's 1957 poetry workshop at the San Francisco Public Library was called "Poetry as Magic"; on the questionnaire Spicer asked his students to fill out for entrance to the seminar, Spicer told his prospective students: "Invent a dream in which you appear as a poet." George Stanley told Robin Blaser that Spicer would also give the assignment, "Create a Universe." Spicer also wrote a poem in 1957 for Stanley called "The Ballad of the Little Girl Who Invented a Universe" that rings even swifter changes on its five or six keywords (Spicer, *Collected Books,* 356, 353, 14). He is willing to punish the word—in that same year, in his first serially organized book, *After Lorca,* he writes to his dead compatriot:

   > See how weak prose is. I invent a word like invention. These paragraphs could be translated, transformed by a chain of fifty poets in fifty languages, and they still would be temporary, untrue, unable to yield the substance of a single image. Prose invents—poetry discloses. (*Collected Books,* 15)

   But in the distinction Spicer draws between "invention" and "disclosure" in his letter to Lorca, the distinction between prose and poetry, it's the description of "prose" that most closely describes Spicer's poetic practice, not least his transposition and transformation-in-a-series. In an adoring poem to Jim Alexander, a young writer whose return to California he eagerly awaited in 1959, Spicer writes of the two of them, in a mythologizing third person:

   > They invented a game which was more complicated than bridge or chess or football which was played with gum and chalk and a piece of common wrapping paper. (*Collected Poetry,* 236)

   Talking to the dead, Spicer feels shy about invention; with his friends, it seems a first step to poetic "disclosure," to the moment of magic. The word "invent" and its variants appear almost forty times in the *Collected Poetry of Jack*

Spicer edited by Peter Gizzi and Kevin Killian, almost always in the context of poetic "gaming."

6. Spicer's anti-Semitic language is different from the archetypical American poetic anti-Semitism, that is, Pound's: it is rare, it is not central to his poetics, is it not obsessive, and it is part of an "underwebbing" of self-hatred in which Black people and gay people are abjected from the human, as in this passage from a collegiate short story, which Kevin Killian quotes in "Spicer and the Mattachine," a scene of dancing in a gay bar:

> Somebody tell me that these people are human. That's silly. They are not human they are homosexual. Jews are not human either, nor Negroes, nor cripples. No one is human that doesn't feel human. None of us here feel human. (n.p.)

   Still, you wish he could have risen above it.

7. Michael Snediker has written beautifully on *Billy the Kid,* arguing that the serial form is especially well suited to Spicer's sense of Billy as serially reproducible. See Snediker, "Jack Spicer's *Billy the Kid.*"
8. For the founding articulations of this idea, see Chomsky 43–44.
9. For some wonderful details from Adams's play, see Ellingham and Killian 90–92.
10. Anita Sokolsky argues that it is not only the formal play of Spicer's sentences, but his hostility to personage, that prefigures the antireferential—and antihumanist—strain of Language writing. See Sokolsky, "Character Assassination."
11. Gizzi notes that he gets the phrase "termite art" from the artist and film critic Manny Farber, who writes in a 1962 essay called "White Elephant Art vs. Termite Art," "Termite-tapeworm-fungus-moss art goes always forward eating its own boundaries, and, like as not, leaves nothing in its path other than the signs of eager, industrious, unkempt activity." See Farber, *Negative Space,* 135.
12. I am grateful to Ryan Dirks for first pointing out this poem to me.
13. Frederick Newmeyer has written the best overview of this transition in American linguistics; his *Politics of Linguistics* rehearses the terms and follows the consequences of the Chomskian revolution. For an excellent account of the relationship of the Language poets to the universalism of linguistics, see Oren Izenberg, "Language Poetry and Collective Life." Izenberg is especially sharp on how the Language poets resisted what seemed to them a distressingly decontextualized notion of universal competence, while nonetheless importing the idea from this moment in linguistic theory. Hejinian's remarks in "The Rejection of Closure" are a good example of this.
14. In a fascinating and somewhat frightening essay on Althusser's use of Pascal, Thomas Pepper notes that elsewhere in the "Ideological State Apparatus"

essay Althusser distinguishes in passing among different "modalities" of materiality that may be at work, in overlapping ways, in the creation of the ideological subject. Pepper (while ecstatically praising Althusser as his father and teacher) refers to Althusser's distinction among modally different "materialities" as a "scattering" of materiality. This puts me in mind of Palmer's use of Spicer's quote from "A Textbook of Poetry"—"Not as a gesture of contempt for the scattered nature of reality"—where Spicer's stashing-away of "reality," like the ashes of D. H. Lawrence scattered through a ton of concrete, walks the line between protecting poetry from capture by mass culture and trapping poetic material in a cultic counterenclosure of poetic purity and loyalty games. Spicer seems to have arrived in this uncomfortable place; Palmer is historicizing it. See Pepper, "Kneel and You Will Believe."

15. See Daniel 5:3–8. Belshazzar, the Babylonian king, had made items stolen from the Temple in Jerusalem into vessels for wining and dining; but a disembodied hand appears to him and writes a prophecy he cannot read. Verse 8: "Then came in all the king's wise men: but they could not read the writing, nor make known to the king the interpretation thereof."

Bibliography

Adorno, Theodor W. *Aesthetic Theory.* Trans. Robert Hullot-Kentor. Minneapolis: University of Minnesota Press, 1996.

———. *Kant's Critique of Pure Reason.* Trans. Rodney Livingstone. Stanford: Stanford University Press, 2001.

———. "Lyric Poetry and Society." Trans. Bruce Mayo. *The Adorno Reader.* Ed. Brian O'Connor. London: Blackwell, 2000.

Althusser, Louis. "Ideology and Ideological State Apparatus (Notes toward an Investigation)." *Lenin and Philosophy and Other Essays.* Trans. Ben Brewster. New York: Monthly Review Press, 1971.

———. *Negative Dialectics.* Trans. E. B. Ashton. New York: Continuum Publishing Company, 1973.

Altieri, Charles. *The Art of Twentieth-Century American Poetry.* Malden, Mass.: Blackwell, 2006.

———. *Painterly Abstraction in Modernist American Poetry.* University Park: Pennsylvania State University Press, 1995.

———. *Self and Sensibility in Contemporary American Poetry.* Cambridge: Cambridge University Press, 1984.

Ashbery, John. *Collected Poems, 1956–1987.* New York: Library of America, 2008.

Association fédérative générale des étudiants de Strasbourg (Mustapha Khayati). *On the Poverty of Student Life Considered in Its Economic, Political, Psychological, Sexual, and Particularly Intellectual Aspects, and a Modest Proposal for Its Remedy.* Pamphlet. Trans. T. J. Clark and Donald Nicholson-Smith.

Attridge, Derek, Geoff Bennington, and Robert Young, eds. *Post-Structuralism and the Question of History.* Cambridge: Cambridge University Press, 1989.

Auden, W. H. *A Certain World.* New York: Viking, 1970.

———. *New Year Letter.* London: Faber and Faber, 1941.

———. *Prose, Volume II: 1939–1948. The Complete Works of W. H. Auden.* Princeton: Princeton University Press, 2002.

———. *Prose, Volume III: 1949–1955. The Complete Works of W. H. Auden.* Princeton: Princeton University Press, 2002.

———. Review of Alvah C. Bessie, *Men in Battle: A Story of Americans in Spain. Common Sense* (Jan. 1940). Reprinted in *Prose, Volume II,* 39–41.

———. *Selected Poems.* Ed. Edward Mendelson. New York: Vintage, 2007.

Auerbach, Erich. *Literary Language and Its Public in Late Latin Antiquity and in the Middle Ages.* Trans. Ralph Manheim. Princeton: Princeton University Press, 1965.

———. *Mimesis: The Representation of Reality in Western Literature.* Trans. Willard Trask. Princeton: Princeton University Press, 1968.

Baker, Houston. *Blues, Ideology, and Afro-American Literature: A Vernacular Theory.* Chicago: University of Chicago Press, 1987.

Baraka, Amiri. "Black Bourgeoisie." *Harper's* Apr. 1965: 158.

———. *Transbluesency: The Selected Poems of Amiri Baraka / LeRoi Jones, 1961–1995.* New York: Marsilio, 1995.

Beaud, Michel. *A History of Capitalism, 1500–2000.* Trans. Tom Dickman and Anny Lefebvre. New York: Monthly Review Press, 2001.

Bell, Daniel. *The Cultural Contradictions of Capitalism.* New York: Basic Books, 1978.

Bercovitch, Sacvan, and Cyrus R. K. Patell, eds. *The Cambridge History of American Literature.* Vol. 5: *Poetry and Criticism, 1900–1950.* Cambridge: Cambridge University Press, 2003.

Bernstein, Michael André. *The Tale of the Tribe: Ezra Pound and the Modern Verse Epic.* Princeton: Princeton University Press, 1990.

Berry, Wendell. "Faustian Economics: Hell Hath No Limits." *Harper's* May 2008: 35.

———. *The Mad Farmer Poems.* Berkeley, Calif.: Counterpoint Press, 2008.

Boone, Bruce. "For Jack Spicer: And a Truth Element." *Social Text* 7 (Spring–Summer 1983): 120.

Bramwell, Anna. *The Fading of the Greens: The Decline of Environmental Politics in the West.* New Haven: Yale University Press, 1994.

Buell, Lawrence. *The Environmental Imagination: Thoreau, Nature Writing, and the Formation of American Culture.* Cambridge, Mass.: Harvard University Press, 1996.

Bush, Ronald. *The Genesis of Ezra Pound's The Cantos.* Princeton: Princeton University Press, 1976.

"A Canto for Ezra Pound." Collaborative poem published in *Commonweal* (Berkeley, California), 2003, n.p.

Césaire, Aimé. *Notebook of a Return to My Native Land.* Ed. Clayton Eshleman and Annette Smith. Middletown, Conn.: Wesleyan University Press, 2001.

Chomsky, Noam. *Syntactic Structures.* Berlin: Mouton de Gruyter, 1957.

Clover, Joshua. *Autumn of the System: Poetry and Finance Capital.* Paper delivered at the annual meeting of the Modern Language Association, San Francisco, 28 Dec. 2008.

———. "A Form Adequate to History." *Paideuma* 37.1–2 (2010).

———. *The Matrix.* London: British Film Institute, 2004.

Conte, Joseph M. *Unending Design: The Forms of Postmodern Poetry.* Ithaca, N.Y.: Cornell University Press, 1991.

Copeland, Rita. *Rhetoric, Hermeneutics, and Translation in the Middle Ages.* Cambridge: Cambridge University Press, 1995.

Crunden, Robert Morse. *American Salons: Encounters with European Modernism, 1885–1917.* Oxford: Oxford University Press, 1993.

Cudahy, Brian J. *Rails under the Mighty Hudson: The Story of the Hudson Tubes, the Pennsy Tunnels, and Manhattan Transfer.* New York: Fordham University Press, 2002.

Curtius, Ernst Robert. *European Literature and the Latin Middle Ages.* Trans. Willard R. Trask. Princeton: Princeton University Press, 1991.

Davies, Kevin. *Comp.* Washington, D.C.: Edge Books, 2000.

———. *The Golden Age of Paraphernalia.* Washington, D.C.: Edge Books, 2008.

Denning, Michael. *The Cultural Front: The Laboring of American Culture in the Twentieth Century.* London: Verso, 1997.

Derrida, Jacques. "From Restricted to General Economy: A Hegelianism without Reserve." *Writing and Difference.* Trans. Alan Bass. Chicago: University of Chicago Press, 1980.

DuBois, Andrew, and Frank Lentricchia. "Modernist Lyric in the Culture of Capital." Bercovitch and Patell 9–178.

Dunn, Brad, and Daniel Hood. *New York: The Unknown City.* Vancouver: Arsenal Pulp, 2004.

Eliot, T. S. *Collected Poems, 1909–1962.* San Diego: Harcourt Brace Jovanovich, 1971.

Ellingham, Lewis, and Kevin Killian. *Poet Be Like God: Jack Spicer and the San Francisco Renaissance.* Middletown, Conn.: Wesleyan University Press, 1998.

Ellman, Maud. "Ezra Pound: The Erasure of History." Attridge, Bennington, and Young 244–262.

Farber, Manny. *Negative Space: Manny Farber on the Movies.* New York: Da Capo Press, 1998.

Fletcher, Angus. *A New Theory for American Poetry: Democracy, the Environment, and the Future of Imagination.* Cambridge, Mass.: Harvard University Press, 2004.

Ford, Mark. *John Ashbery in Conversation with Mark Ford.* London: Between the Lines, 2003.

Ford, Simon. *The Situationist International: A User's Guide.* London: Black Dog, 2005.

Gabriele, Matthew, and Jace Stuckey, eds. *The Legend of Charlemagne in the Middle Ages: Power, Faith, and Crusade.* New York: Palgrave, 2008.

Ginsberg, Allen. *Selected Poems, 1947–1995.* New York: HarperCollins, 1996.

Graff, Gerald. *Professing Literature: An Institutional History.* 20th anniv. ed. Chicago: University of Chicago Press, 2007.

Halpern, Richard. *The Poetics of Primitive Accumulation: English Renaissance Culture and the Genealogy of Capital.* Ithaca, N.Y.: Cornell University Press, 1991.

Harvey, David. *A Brief History of Neoliberalism.* Oxford: Oxford University Press, 2005.

Hejinian, Lyn. *The Cell.* Los Angeles: Sun and Moon, 1992.

———. *The Language of Inquiry.* Berkeley: University of California Press, 2000.

Herndon, Jim. *Manroot* 10. San Francisco, 1974.

Hobsbawm, Eric. *The Age of Extremes: A History of the World, 1914–1991.* New York: Vintage, 1994.

Horkheimer, Max, and Theodor W. Adorno. *Dialectic of Enlightenment: Philosophical Fragments.* Trans. Edmund Jephcott. Stanford: Stanford University Press, 2002.

Howard, Richard. Review of Ashbery, *The Double Dream of Spring.* Ford, *Ashbery,* 150.

Huyssen, Andreas. *After the Great Divide: Modernism, Mass Culture, Postmodernism.* Bloomington: Indiana University Press, 1986.

Irvine, Martin. *The Making of Textual Culture: "Grammatica" and Literary Theory, 350–1100.* Cambridge: Cambridge University Press, 2006.

Izenberg, Oren. "Language Poetry and Collective Life." *Critical Inquiry* 30 (Autumn 2003): 132–159.

Jackson, Virginia. *Dickinson's Misery: A Theory of Lyric Reading.* Princeton: Princeton University Press, 2005.

Jacobs, Jane. *The Death and Life of Great American Cities.* New York: Random House, 1993.

Jauss, Han-Robert. "Modernity and Literary Tradition." Trans. Christian Thorne. *Critical Inquiry* 31 (Winter 2005): 329–364.

Jay, Martin. *Marxism and Totality: The Adventures of a Concept from Lukács to Habermas.* Berkeley: University of California Press, 1986.

Killian, Kevin. "Spicer and the Mattachine." Forthcoming in Vincent, *After Spicer.*

Klein, Naomi. *The Shock Doctrine: The Rise of Disaster Capitalism.* New York: Metropolitan Books, 2007.

Kristeva, Julia. *Revolution in Poetic Language.* Trans. Margaret Waller. New York: Columbia University Press, 1984.

Kutulas, Judy. *The Long War: The Intellectual People's Front and Anti-Stalinism, 1930–1940.* Durham, N.C.: Duke University Press, 1995.

LaFeber, Walter. *America, Russia, and the Cold War, 1945–2006.* New York: McGraw-Hill, 2006.

Lederer, Katy. "A Nietzschean Revival." *Crowd* 5.1–2 (2005).

Lolordo, Nick. "Charting the Flow: Positioning John Ashbery." *Contemporary Literature* 42.1 (2001): 750–774.

Longenbach, James. "Ashbery and the Individual Talent." *American Literary History* 9 (1997): 103–127.

———. *Wallace Stevens: The Plain Sense of Things.* Oxford: Oxford University Press, 1991.

Loomis, Roger Sherman. *The Development of Arthurian Romance.* New York: W. W. Norton, 1970.

Lucier, Alvin. "I Am Sitting in a Room." 1969. *UbuWeb Sound.* Audio. Web. 11 Apr. 2009.

Malkiel, Burton. *A Random Walk down Wall Street: The Time-Tested Strategy for Successful Investing.* New York: W. W. Norton, 1973.

Martin, Randy. *The Financialization of Daily Life.* Philadelphia: Temple University Press, 2002.

Masters, Edgar Lee. *Spoon River Anthology.* New York: Penguin Classics, 2008.

Meacham, Jon, and Evan Thomas. "We Are All Socialists Now." *Newsweek* 7 Feb. 2009. Web. 21 Mar. 2009.

Mendelson, Edward. *Early Auden.* New York: Farrar, Straus, and Giroux, 2000.

Moxley, Jennifer. *Clampdown.* New York: Flood, 2009.

Murphy, Michael. "Neoclassicism, Late Modernism, and W. H. Auden's 'New Year Letter.'" *Cambridge Quarterly* 33 (2004): 101–118.

Nadel, Ira B., ed. *The Cambridge Companion to Ezra Pound.* Cambridge: Cambridge University Press, 1999.

Nancy, Jean-Luc. "Literary Communism." *The Inoperable Community.* Trans. Christopher Fynsk. Minneapolis: Minnesota University Press, 1991.

Nelson, Cary. *Repression and Recovery: Modern American Poetry and the Politics of Cultural Memory, 1910–1945.* Madison: University of Wisconsin Press, 1989.

———. *Revolutionary Memory: Recovering the Poetry of the American Left.* New York: Routledge, 2001.

Newmeyer, Frederick. *The Politics of Linguistics.* Chicago: University of Chicago Press, 1988.

Nicholls, Peter. *Modernisms: A Literary Guide.* Berkeley: University of California Press, 1995.

Nocera, Joe. "Risk Mismanagement." *New York Times* 2 Jan. 2009. Web. 23 Mar. 2009.

O'Hara, Frank. *Selected Poems.* Ed. Mark Ford. New York: Knopf, 2008.

Ong, Walter J. *Orality and Literacy: The Technologization of the Word.* New York: Methuen, 1982.

———. *Ramus, Method, and the Decay of Dialogue.* Chicago: University of Chicago Press, 2004.

Oppen, George. *New Collected Poems.* Ed. Michael Davidson. New York: New Directions, 2002.

Palmer, Michael. *Codes Appearing: Poems 1979–1988.* New York: New Directions, 2001.

Pepper, Thomas. "Kneel and You Will Believe." *Yale French Studies* 88 (1995): 27–41.

Perelman, Bob, ed. *Writing/Talks.* Carbondale: Southern Illinois University Press, 1985.

Perloff, Marjorie. *The Dance of the Intellect: Studies in the Poetry of the Pound Tradition.* Evanston, Ill.: Northwestern University Press, 1985.

———. *The Poetics of Indeterminacy: Rimbaud to Cage.* Princeton: Princeton University Press, 1981.

———.*Wittgenstein's Ladder: Poetic Language and the Strangeness of the Ordinary.* Chicago: University of Chicago Press, 1996.

Pound, Ezra. *ABC of Reading.* New York: New Directions, 1960.

———. *The Cantos of Ezra Pound.* London: Faber and Faber, 1975.

———. *Pavannes and Divisions.* New York: Knopf, 1918.

———. *Personae: The Shorter Poems of Ezra Pound.* Ed. Lea Baechler and A. Walton Litz. New York: New Directions, 1990.

Rancière, Jacques. Interview. By Fulvia Carnevale and John Kelsey. *ArtForum* Mar. 2007.

Rankine, Claudia. *Don't Let Me Be Lonely: An American Lyric.* Saint Paul, Minn.: Graywolf, 2004.

Ransom, John Crowe. "Prometheus in Straits." *Modern American Poetry.* University of Illinois. Web. 3 July 2009.

Redman, Tim. "Pound's Politics and Economics." Nadel 249–263.

Rexroth, Kenneth. *The Complete Poems of Kenneth Rexroth.* Ed. Sam Hamill and Bradford Morrow. Port Townsend, WA: Copper Canyon, 2003.

Rich, Adrienne. *Arts of the Possible.* New York: W. W. Norton, 2001.

———. *Dark Fields of the Republic.* New York: W. W. Norton, 1995.

———. *Diving into the Wreck.* New York: W. W. Norton, 1973.

———. *The Dream of a Common Language.* New York: W. W. Norton, 1978.

———. *Midnight Salvage.* New York: W. W. Norton, 1999.

Riley, Peter. "The Narratives of the Holy Grail." *boundary 2* 6.1 (Autumn 1977): 163–190.

Ronda, Margaret. *Disenchanted Georgics: The Aesthetics of Labor in American Poetry.* Diss. University of California, Berkeley, 2009.

Rukeyser, Muriel. *Selected Poems.* Ed. Adrienne Rich. New York: Library of America, 2004.

Sandburg, Carl. *Collected Poems.* New York: Henry Holt, 1916.

Schiller, Friedrich. *On the Aesthetic Education of Man: In a Series of Letters.* Trans. Elizabeth M. Wilkinson and L. A. Willoughby. Oxford: Oxford University Press, 1967.

Segal, David. "Our Love Affair with Malls Is on the Rocks." *New York Times* 31 Jan. 2009. Web. 21 Mar. 2009.

Shannon, Joshua. *The Disappearance of Objects: New York Art and the Rise of the Postmodern City.* New Haven: Yale University Press, 2009.

Shell, Marc. *The Economy of Literature.* Baltimore: Johns Hopkins University Press, 1978.

Shoptaw, John. *On the Outside Looking Out: John Ashbery's Poetry.* Cambridge, Mass.: Harvard University Press, 1995.

Shutt, Harry. *The Trouble with Capitalism: An Enquiry into the Causes of Global Economic Failure.* London: Zed Books, 1998.

Sieburth, Richard. "In Pound We Trust: The Economy of Poetry / The Poetry of Economics." *Critical Inquiry* 14.1 (Autumn 1987): 142–172.

Silliman, Ron. *The New Sentence.* New York: Roof Books, 1987.

———. "Spicer's Language." Perelman 166–191.

Smith, Stan, ed. *The Cambridge Companion to W. H. Auden.* Cambridge: Cambridge University Press, 2004.

Snediker, Michael. "Jack Spicer's *Billy the Kid:* Beyond the Singular Personal." Forthcoming in Vincent, *After Spicer.*

Snyder, Gary. *Axe Handles.* Washington, D.C.: Shoemaker and Hoard, 1983.

Sokolsky, Anita. "Character Assassination in the Poetry of Jack Spicer." Forthcoming in Vincent, *After Spicer.*

Spicer, Jack. *The Collected Books of Jack Spicer.* Ed. Robin Blaser. Santa Rosa, Calif.: Black Sparrow Press, 1975.

———. *My Vocabulary Did This to Me: The Collected Poetry of Jack Spicer.* Ed. Peter Gizzi and Kevin Killian. Berkeley: University of California Press, 2008.

Stein, Gertrude. *The Autobiography of Alice B. Toklas.* New York: Vintage, 1990.

Stevens, Wallace. *Collected Poems.* New York: Vintage, 1990.

Surette, Leon. *Pound in Purgatory: From Economic Radicalism to Anti-Semitism.* Urbana: University of Illinois Press, 1999.

Szalay, Michael. *New Deal Modernism: American Literature and the Invention of the Welfare State.* Durham, N.C.: Duke University Press, 2000.

Tabb, William. *New York City and the Urban Fiscal Crisis.* New York: Monthly Review Press, 1982.

Taleb, Nassim Nicholas. *The Black Swan: The Impact of the Highly Improbable.* New York: Random House, 2007.

Terrell, Carroll F. *A Companion to the Cantos of Ezra Pound.* Berkeley: University of California Press, in cooperation with the University of Maine at Orono, 1993.

Trilling, Lionel. *The Liberal Imagination.* New York: Harcourt, 1979.

Tufte, Edward R. *The Cognitive Style of PowerPoint.* Cheshire, Conn.: Graphics Press, 2003.

Vance, Eugene. *From Topic to Tale: Logic and Narrativity in the Middle Ages.* Minneapolis: Minnesota University Press, 1987.

Vincent, John Emil, ed. *After Spicer.* Forthcoming.

———. "Before *After Spicer.*" Forthcoming in Vincent, *After Spicer.*

———. *John Ashbery and You.* Athens: University of Georgia Press, 2008.

Wasley, Aidan. "The 'Gay Apprentice': Ashbery, Auden, and a Portrait of the Artist as a Young Critic." *Contemporary Literature* 43.4 (Winter 2002): 687.

Watten, Barrett. *Total Syntax.* Carbondale: Southern Illinois University Press, 1985.

Wroe, Nicholas. "Parallel Lines." *The Guardian* 23 Apr. 2005: 20.

Zukofsky, Louis. *A.* Baltimore: Johns Hopkins University Press, 1978.

Acknowledgments

Many people, and not a few institutions, have helped make writing this book possible. I am grateful to the English Departments at the University of California, Berkeley, and The Johns Hopkins University for time in which to work on this book. I deeply appreciate the questions and comments of audiences at Rutgers, Columbia, Yale, and New York Universities, as well as at the "Poetry of the 1970s" conference at the University of Maine, where I delivered excerpts from the book in progress. A portion of Chapter 2, first delivered as a paper at the Orono conference, appears online through the conference's website, and a small part of Chapter 3 appeared in a special issue of *Textual Practice* under the title "Affect, Performativity, and Actually Existing Poetry" in spring 2011 (Volume 25, Number 2). Meanwhile I am grateful to these people and organizations for their permission to reprint the following poems in their entirety: the editors of *CROWD* magazine, for permission to reprint Katy Lederer's poem "A Nietzschean Revival"; Lyn Hejinian, for permission to reprint her poem "In the dark sky there / are constellations" from *The Cell;* and Wesleyan University Press, for permission to reprint four poems from Jack Spicer's *My Vocabulary Did This to Me: The Collected Poetry of Jack Spicer:* "Sporting Life," "Thing Language," "Postscript," and "Transformations."

In 2007–2008 I was a fellow at the Society for the Humanities at Cornell University, and I would like to thank Brett de Bary, the director of the Society, the staff at the A. D. White House, the students in my "Poetry and Totality" seminar, and the members of my fellowship group for the productive and intellectually engaging time I spent at Cornell. Kevin Killian, John Emil Vincent, Michael Snediker, and Anita Sokolsky kindly allowed me access to wonderful material on Jack Spicer prior to its publication in forthcoming volumes, and Brandon Brown supplied me with a hard-to-find copy of Spicer and Duncan's "Canto for Ezra Pound." I am grateful to Lindsay Waters at Harvard University Press for taking an interest in this book, and to Hannah Wong for all her help getting it into print. Joshua Clover has been a tireless and inspiring interlocutor from the moment of this book's first inkling; his intelligence is everywhere in these pages. And Rob Hardies—well—he has held me. This book is for him.

Index

Harvard University Press is a member of Green Press Initiative (greenpressinitiative.org), a nonprofit organization working to help publishers and printers increase their use of recycled paper and decrease their use of fiber derived from endangered forests. This book was printed on recycled paper containing 30% post-consumer waste and processed chlorine free.